Praise for Kayleen Reusser's books:

We Fought to Win: American World War II Veterans Share Their Stories (Book 1, World War II Legacies)
"This book documents the experiences and sacrifices of Hoosier veterans who are a part of The Greatest Generation."

Christopher Wiljer, librarian, Allen County Public Library

**

They Did It for Honor: Stories of American WWII Veterans (Book 2, World War II Legacies)
"The information shared from the hearts of 34 World War Two Veterans is simply stunning.
Curtis Rose, Vietnam veteran

**

We Gave Our Best: American WWII Veterans Tell Their Stories (Book 3, World War II Legacies)
"The stories are written in short, easy-to-read biographies and are eye-witness accounts ranging from their wartime experiences to heartwarming memories."

Shana Neuenschwander, librarian, Jay County Public Library

**

D1593221

D-Day: Soldiers, Sailors and Airmen Tell about Normandy (Book 1, World War II Insider)
"The author has pulled from first-hand stories of those that were there … (to tell) what it was like to be among the first to wade upon the shores of Europe for the end of Nazi terrorism."
Harold Wolf, Amazon Top 500 Reviewer

**

It Was Our War Too: Youth in the Shadows of WWII
"School children would get a good idea of what it was like to be a child during wartime, and how it affected these individuals as adults."
Joy Neal Kidney, author of Leora's Letters

Captured!

Stories of American World War II Prisoners of War

by

Kayleen Reusser

First published in the United States by Kayleen Reusser Media. Printed in the United States.

KayleenReusser.com

ISBN: 978-1-7325172-4-0

Cover illustration by Kayleen Reusser. Printed in the United States of America

Dedication

This book is dedicated to my parents -- Evelyn Joan Brewer who has taught me about patience, forbearance and courage throughout my life and especially in recent times; Forace Hale Brewer who loved learning about World War II.

I also thank my family of whom I am very proud and love very much. My husband John is an Air Force veteran who has always supported me. I'm proud of being his wife. Love always,

Contents

Introduction

At times, most of us have felt deprived and out of sorts when forced -- due to health, finances, situations out of our control -- to cut back on something we enjoy. If we can't visit a favorite restaurant, go on vacation, or attend a sporting event, we think it's a hardship. I've felt the same.

After working on these stories about prisoners of war (POWs) of World War II, my perspective has changed. I've realized the challenges we face in the 21st century are small compared to what these men and their families experienced.

Sixteen million Americans served in World War II. Of these, more than 120,000 lived out part of the war behind barbed wire. In the European theater, 93,941 Americans were held as prisoners of war (POWs).

Of the 27,000 Americans taken prisoner by the Japanese, a shocking 40 percent died in captivity, according to the U.S. Congressional Research Service. That compares with just one percent of American prisoners who died in German POW camps.

The courage it took to invade enemy territory, only to be captured and made a prisoner for months, sometimes years, enduring starvation, terrible diseases and cruelty, is hard to hear. But each story offers a perspective and message about life that is badly needed. That message is the importance of resilience and pressing on.

One factor especially poignant to me was how young these men were -- some still in their teens! They not only shared prison camp experiences, but a couple shared birthdays!

It was thrilling during my research to find letters written by the POWs to families and letters from their families to them. Excerpts are reprinted here with original spelling, slang and punctuation for authenticity.

One story is different in this book.

Of the hundreds of World War II veterans whose stories I've recorded, all were interviewed by me. That is true for this volume -- except for one.

Granville ('Grant') E. Workman lived in my hometown of Bluffton, Indiana, for much of his life. He died in 1998 before I began interviewing veterans. I never knew him.

After he returned home from WWII, Mr. Workman wrote a journal about his time as a soldier on the Bataan Death March and three years in Japanese POW camps.

That journal was shared with me by Grant's daughter, Judy Johnson. It was a fascinating read with details that only a young soldier who had run through the jungle, gun in hand, not knowing if he would run into an enemy camp, could provide.

Grant Workman's journal ends with his time in a Prisoner of War camp in the Philippines. He also was one of the few Americans who were part of slave labor in Japan on a railroad project in the spring of 1945, according to a reference he made in a document.

With some edits for spelling and grammar the journal is provided here in its entirety. It is written in first-person, giving the reader a first-hand view of what it was like to hide from the enemy in the Philippines, survive the Bataan Death March, see the American flag torn down, not once but twice.

Workman and the others existed for years with little food, suffering abuse and nearly dying on more than one occasion. What got them through was a will to survive and belief that they were fighting for a strong country.

Thanks to Grant Workman's daughter, Judy Johnson, for providing me with a copy of the journal, photos, and other vital information.

Thanks to all of the veterans and their families who supported my efforts to put this book together. I hope it will cause all Americans to view our ideals and flag with renewed enthusiasm.

Note: The journal includes several mentions of violence and cruelty. In this age when people want to re-write history and remove "bad" parts, I chose not to sanitize the horrors the soldiers faced.

God bless America!

Background of World War II:

World War II began in 1939 when German troops invaded Poland. In 1940, France and other countries in Europe were taken over by the Nazis.

By 1942, the Nazis under the dictatorship of Adolf Hitler controlled most of Europe. Only England prevailed against numerous bombings of its cities and countryside with much loss of life and destruction.

On December 7, 1941, Japanese military forces attacked the American Navy at Pearl Harbor, Hawaii. During that assault, more than 2,403 Americans sailors died. Within days, the United States Congress had declared war on the Axis Powers – Japan, Germany, and Italy.

The deaths of thousands of sailors and civilians infuriated the American public. Patriotism among the people of America was high. Thousands of men, still in their teens, wanted to serve in the Armed Forces in defense of the United States. They were most often sent to one of two theaters of operation: Europe or the Pacific.

Richard H. Beach – Army Air Corps

Richard Beach crouched low behind snow-covered fallen logs. The area of the Hurtgen Forest where he and a dozen soldiers with the Fourth Infantry had advanced was thought to be filled with German troops.

Upon receiving the signal, the group slowly moved forward. Truth be told, they had no idea in which direction Allied lines were located. It felt like they were plastic ducks in a shooting gallery — easy pickings.

When the group discovered foxholes, they tumbled inside the earthy holes, thankful for cover.

At six by six feet, the foxholes were not much sanctuary but they were better than nothing in the frigid cold weather. One soldier kept lookout.

The group had been sent on reconnaissance for the battle that had begun on the border of Germany and Belgium in September 1944. A guarantee of air support had proven to be false as they had seen no planes, possibly due to low cloud cover.

Beach wiggled his toes inside his GI (government-issue) boots. Not only did the group have to watch for the enemy, they were forced to survive sub-zero temperatures – some of the lowest recorded for that region.

When given the signal to advance, the group reluctantly left their foxholes.

Immediately German soldiers appeared from behind trees, pointing machine guns at the group and barking orders. As the Germans made abrupt gestures with their guns, the Americans who didn't speak the language understood -- they were to toss down their rifles and grenades and walk. Richard Beach tried to still his racing heart. He had never dreamed he would be a prisoner of war.

It was a Beach family tradition to serve one's country. An ancestor of Richard's had served in the Civil War. His father, Perry Beach, had fought in World War I.

But the situation at home had made it difficult for Richard to leave. His father had been recalled to military service and was serving in the Army National Guard Reserves at Fort Knox, Kentucky.

After graduating from high school in 1941, Richard's older brother Clifford had enlisted in the Army Air Corps. That left Richard, 17, to help his mother Luella with three younger siblings and the running of the family's grocery store in Ohio City, Ohio (pop. 800).

On Richard's 18th birthday, the United States government promptly sent him his draft notice. Luella applied for and received a six-month deferment for him to continue to help her.

By April 1944, however, the Army refused to issue another deferment and Richard Beach left for basic training at Fort Robinson near Little Rock, Arkansas. He had hoped to go into the Army Air Corps, but by that time in the war air crew slots were full.

During 13 weeks of basic training, Beach and hundreds of other troops learned to march, run hundreds of miles with full packs on their backs, salute and shoot targets at 500 yards. Besides the grueling demands of learning to look and act like soldiers, the young men dealt with the challenges of heat, dust and sand, while forced to keep their barracks and uniforms clean.

After basic training, Beach was sent to Fort Meade, Maryland, where he boarded the RMS *Queen Mary* for Europe. Dubbed the 'Grey Ghost', the luxury liner converted to a troop ship was thought to be one of the fastest vessels in the world and able to outrun German submarines in the Atlantic Ocean. Thus it had no escort.

The ship arrived safely in Scotland and ventured on to Southampton on England's south coast before heading to France.

Germans capture American soldiers on the western front, December 1944. National Archives.

The battle in Hurtgen Forest that had begun in fall 1944 would continue until mid-December with a German victory at a cost of 33,000 Allied casualties (mostly American) and 28,000 German lives.

That conflict led directly into the Battle of the Bulge, one of the major battles of the war, taking place in Belgium and Germany. It would end with an Allied victory and be a turning point of the war, though again at a cost -- 19,000 soldiers killed in action, 47,500 wounded and 23,000 missing.

Beach and the other American prisoners followed their German captors on a long hike before stopping at a building where they were interrogated individually and given no food.

Beach recalled his Army training of what to do if captured -- recite only name, rank, and serial number. He was shocked when his interrogators switched mid-interview to English. He was even more astonished when his captors supplied personal information about him, including the date of his induction into the Army, presumably obtained through spies.

Beach and 50 American prisoners stayed at a Stalag (abbreviation for Kriegsgefangenen-Mannschafts-Stammlager, meaning 'prison') surrounded by barbed wire. In January 1945 they were forced into boxcars and rode for days without food, little water and poor sanitary conditions. Finally, they arrived at an Allied prison camp near Pilsen in western Czechoslovakia.

It was a squalid existence for the POWs. They were housed on the second floor of a warehouse and given no blankets against the cold, the only heat radiating from a stove in the kitchen on the floor below. Thin mattresses were filled with lice. The men spent much time picking them from their bodies and hair.

Each prisoner was given a work assignment. Beach was part of a crew that dug a tunnel through a mountain where the Germans planned to lay a train track. Returning exhausted to the camp each evening, the prisoners were fed watery soup made from boiled rutabagas and radishes with an occasional slice of sausage thrown in. Only prisoners who worked received food.

Their diet was supplemented by black bread made mostly from straw. After working all day, Beach devoured the often moldy bread to appease his extreme hunger.

It didn't do to complain about anything. On one occasion when Beach mentioned the poor quality of his meal, a guard knocked him to the floor, pointing a rifle in his back.

When not working, Beach peered out a small window in the barracks. He noticed old German machines and trucks and, comparing them to new models used by the Allies, he hoped the Germans were running low on supplies.

The prisoners could hear buzz bombs (rockets) in the distance, but as they had no idea of how the war was progressing, they had no idea of the origin or targets.

At his capture, all of Beach's belongings had been confiscated, including a New Testament Bible issued upon his induction into the Army and a pocket knife. The guards kept the knife but returned the small volume. During his confinement, Beach read the Bible and was comforted by verses of God's promises to always be with His followers.

On rare occasions POWs received letters from friends and family delivered by the Red Cross. Beach knew the international relief agency had sent a telegram to his family, telling of his capture. In turn, Beach wrote letters to his loved ones, uncertain if they were delivered.

Between his Bible reading and thoughts of his loving family, Beach kept his spirits positive. "I always believed I would get home," he said.

When one soldier in Beach's area contracted diphtheria, the group was quarantined for four weeks. This was not a bad thing as it meant a reprieve from work duty with a little food. Beach was thankful to never contract any disease or illness during his captivity.

As spring 1945 approached, rumors about Russian troops in the area circulated throughout the camp. Most German guards deserted their posts at the prison.

When the POWs realized the camp was unguarded, they divided into groups of four and set out on foot, searching for food and freedom. With little idea of which way to go, Beach's group trekked 50 miles northeast toward Prague.

One night his group met some Russian soldiers. They agreed to transport the liberated men in trucks to a spot close to Allied lines.

The journey took three days. When Beach and his group arrived at an Allied field hospital, they were treated for various ailments, including malnutrition and frostbite. Beach's ears, feet, and other parts of his body had suffered great damage which would afflict him throughout his life.

The diet of the POWs was closely monitored in the hospital. Beach never forgot his first meal. "We were fed pancakes!" he said. Not sporting a large body build before his imprisonment, his weight had fallen during his six months as a prisoner from 140 to 105 pounds. He was sprayed with a delousing agent and his filthy clothes replaced with new uniforms.

Richard Beach (right) stands with brother Clifford (left) and father Perry Beach after the war.

Beach was sent to a French hospital to recuperate. He was there on May 8, 1945, when the German army surrendered unconditionally to the Allies at Reims, France.

After several weeks, Beach traveled to Camp Lucky Strike at Le Havre, France for debarkation to the US. As an ex-POW, he received priority and happily boarded a C-47 cargo plane, clutching his New Testament. He had relied on the Bible for comfort and encouragement and vowed to keep the small volume for the rest of his life.

Beach was re-assigned to an army unit in North Carolina. On December 20, 1945, he was discharged from military service at Camp Atterbury in Indianapolis.

Reunited with his family, Beach discovered they had known of his capture from the Red Cross, but not his location. None of his letters reached them.

Anxious to put the horrors of war behind him, Richard Beach purchased half of his family's store from his father. Together, they managed it until 1957 when they closed the business. Richard worked at Aeroquip in Van Wert until retiring in 1986.

In April 1947 he married a childhood friend, Recie Ellinger. They became parents to three children.

Richard's older brother, Clifford, was shot down with the Army Air Corps and also captured, though he escaped to Switzerland, a neutral country. A younger Beach brother would later serve in the Korean War and a grandson in the Marines.

"Before becoming a soldier I thought war was nice," said Richard Beach. "By the time it was over and I saw all of the destruction, there was nothing nice about it."

James Fall – Army Air Corps

On June 10, 1944, 21-year-old Second Lieutenant James 'Jim' Fall crossed the English Channel flying ground support in his P-47 Thunderbolt.

The P-47 sported eight 50-caliber machine guns with 2,000 rounds of ammunition. The plane could carry an additional 108-gallon belly tank, 1,000-pound bomb and bundle of rockets under each wing.

Fall had flown 20 combat missions with the 391st Fighter Squadron, 366th Fighter Group, 9th Air Force. He and dozens of other Thunderbolt pilots, based out of Thruxton, England, had received a mission that morning for Arromanches, France -- search and destroy anything connected with the military.

Fall observed Allied forces far below – American, Canadian and British -- fortifying the beaches of Normandy following the invasion that had occurred on June 6. He had flown on D-Day and was thrilled with the opportunity to be part of such a history-making event.

In the St. Lo area Fall encountered heavy flak. Upon approaching Caen, he felt an alarming thud before his plane suddenly lurched to the right.

Inspecting the aircraft through the window of his cockpit, Fall viewed with horror flames licking the left wing. He had been hit by anti-aircraft ground fire.

Though Fall had heard of other pilots bailing out of planes, the idea always seemed remote. Now he feared his time had arrived.

Making a quick radio call to crew members that he was leaving the formation of four fighters (he found out later the call was never received), Fall gave the wounded bird full throttle to keep it in the air before turning toward the Channel. Parachuting over water away from the battle was preferable to landing on the ground in an inferno.

In P-47 training pilots learned during bailout to roll a plane on its back, release the harness and drop out with parachute over the left side. Otherwise the plane's prop wash could carry a body beneath the tail assembly.

P-47 Thunderbolt stands ready for action.

When Fall attempted a left roll, the plane slipped, due to holes in the wings and a missing right aileron which had been damaged. His attempt with a right roll produced the same disastrous results.

The P-47 continued to take hits. As the cockpit filled with suffocating heat, Fall, terrified of becoming entangled in a burning mass, tried to throw himself over the right side. The powerful prop wash pinned him against the seat back.

The left wing started to wrinkle from the heat. Fall squatted on the seat, put his right foot on the stick and kicked his body as hard as he could away from the tumbling firestorm.

As he flew clear of the burning plane, the air blast ripped the goggles from his face. Temporarily blinded, Fall reached for the chute's ripcord and gave it a tug, thankful when it opened.

Absolute silence. It was a welcome relief from the turbulent engine roar of the Thunderbolt. As his vision slowly returned, Fall recognized the Allied fleet in the Channel. How he wished he could land in their area.

Twinkly lights appeared around him. Enemy gunfire. His descent seemed to accelerate and too soon his body had slammed into the ground. When pain shot up his left leg, Fall knew something had snapped, probably his fibula.

For a few moments he lay in agony. Then, opening his eyes, he glimpsed the stony faces of a group of young boys, each holding a gun on him. Fall knew his flying days were over.

The teens were from the 12th Hitlerjugend Panzer Division. They appeared highly trained and determined as they disarmed Fall and motioned for him to walk.

Limping as fast as he could, Fall passed under camouflage netting covering huge artillery guns. They were targets he and other pilots would like to have fired on.

As the group passed near a house, Fall spied two little girls. They reminded him of his two young sisters at home in Indiana. June and Carol were safe while these children lived in the midst of chaos and death. Fall emptied candy from his pockets and handed it to the children who stared at him with wide eyes.

Fall (standing, far right) poses with members of 391st Fighter Squadron, 366th Fighter Group days in a photo taken before his plane is shot down.

The Nazi teens marched Fall to Chateau de Marcelet near Rosel, France. The elegant home served as a Luftwaffe headquarters. During a search, Fall's cigarettes and lighter were confiscated.

He was interrogated by high-ranking Luftwaffe officers. According to the rules of war in the Geneva Convention, as specified for POWs, Fall was obliged to share only name, rank, and serial number.

Unable to extract additional information, the Nazis told Fall in English, "We will throw you in the cooler for a few days to think about it, then we will talk to you again. If you still refuse to cooperate, we will turn you over to the Gestapo and they will shoot you."

The Gestapo was the greatly feared official secret police of Nazi Germany and German-occupied Europe.

For several hours Fall was kept outside in a barbed wire pen with other POWs before turned over to the Wehrmacht, land forces of the German military.

they put him in a cell in solitary confinement and gave him little water and no food. Fall's left leg throbbed at the break. Between spasms, he longed for his family and home.

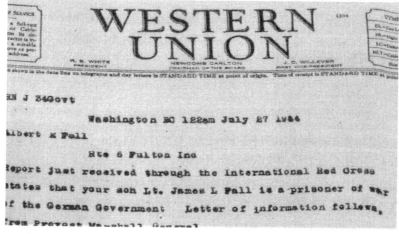

Telegram sent to James Fall's family by the United States government, relaying his status as a prisoner of war.

After graduating from Fulton High School in Indiana in 1941, Fall had enrolled at Manchester College, planning to study veterinary science.

Like most young men after the attack at Pearl Harbor, he wanted to volunteer for the military. His father, Albert Fall, however, refused to sign the form for his son to join.

Note: At the beginning of the war a male had to be 21 years old or have a parent's written permission to enlist in the military. That requirement quickly dropped to 18 years of age.

Albert Fall had served in World War I as an air corps mechanic with the 98th Aero Squadron. Perhaps he didn't want his son to see war up close.

Eventually he relented, offering his son the option of joining the military after he had finished a year of college. Jim Fall agreed to wait, enlisting in the Army Air Corps on his first available day -- July 1, 1942.

Fall completed flight training at a number of sites around the country: San Antonio; Victory Field, Vernon, Texas; Enid Army Air Base; Foster Field, Victoria Texas; Tallahassee and Perry Air Force Base, Perry, Florida.

Several applicants 'washed out' (failed) the phases of training. Jim Fall felt great pride upon receiving his wings as a pilot.

Before leaving the United States in spring 1944, he and Ethel Mae Swank of Rochester, Indiana, had become engaged. She owned a beautician shop in Peru, Indiana.

Upon arriving at Thruxton, Fall was almost too busy to think about home as the 366th was immediately put to work. Objectives of the 9th Air Force in England were to:

- destroy enemy air power in the air and on the ground
- disrupt enemy lines of supply and communication
- support Allied ground forces.

The Americans flew day missions while the British flew at night. Fall supported other pilots' efforts as their wing man and sometimes flew escort for bombers. The Allies targeted train yards, bridges, ammunition dumps and airfields, anything to deter combative efforts of the Nazis.

The enemy struck back aggressively with anti-aircraft fire. On one strafing mission Fall's plane was damaged but he managed to fly back to base, unharmed.

During the days of his imprisonment, Fall felt near the depths of despair and more frightened than he had been in his life. He wondered if he would ever see Ethel Mae or any member of his family again.

A few days later, Fall was put into a wood-burning dump truck that was part of a convoy. Though the group kept to back roads, Allied P-47s spied the group and strafed them. The roar of planes with their clatter of 50-caliber machine guns, explosions and resulting fires in several of the trucks terrified the Germans. They slammed on the brakes and threw themselves into ditches beside the road.

Alone in the truck bed, Fall dropped to the road on his good leg before rolling to the ditch and falling in.

As the raid continued, screams of injured and dying men surrounded Fall who was convinced he would be killed.

By the time the planes left, eight of the 10 trucks were destroyed. Fall and the others were covered with dirt but unharmed.

Ordered to climb aboard a drivable truck, Fall rode with his captors to the French city of Chartres. His captors locked Fall inside a cell in an ancient castle used as a Wehrmacht headquarters.

James Fall's photo as a POW as taken by the Germans.

Cobwebs fluttered across Fall's face and the room smelled mossy as he dropped to the floor. Thick stone walls, cold and damp, allowed a small amount of light through a tiny barred window.

When a German doctor took him to a hospital, Fall hoped to receive treatment for his injured leg. Instead, he was shoved into another dirty room with 20 Canadian POWs, all wounded. The men lay on a bare wooden floor with no medical attention and little food and water.

The Canadians told Fall he should claim to be from Chicago. Apparently, the Germans believed the city was full of gangsters. Fall did as they recommended, but the deception afforded no closer attention.

After a few days, ambulatory prisoners were moved to the top floor of the famous Chartres Cathedral. Built in 1220 with two towering spires and flying buttresses, the cathedral had a majestic presence.

The prisoners' only idea of the building's beauty existed in the stunning fresco artwork of the vaulted ceiling of the huge room in which they were imprisoned. Through one tall, narrow window, the prisoners could see a grass landing strip outside. Hangars sheltering Focke-Wulf 190s (FW-190s) planes lay hidden in the hillside.

The single-seat, single-engine fighters designed in the late 1930s were widely used during the war and considered one of the Luftwaffe's workhorses.

One day, the POWs were thrilled to see P-47s tailing the FW-190s to their lair. American pilots strafed the hidden hangars and many of the enemy planes burst into flames.

The imprisoned men in the garret of the Chartres Cathedral cheered.

The Ninth Air Force participated in Egypt and Libya, Tunisia and invasions of Sicily and Italy. The 9th also fought at Normandy through the rest of the war.

A German guard, angry at the show of enthusiasm, entered their room, letting loose bursts from his gun. The beautiful, centuries-old fresco on the ceiling shattered, pieces flying. The invaluable artwork was gone forever.

After several days, Fall and the other POWs were pushed on to a truck for another move. At the outskirts of the city French people dug through rubble from a recent bombing. As the truck slowed, an older woman, spying the POWs, held up the 'V for Victory' sign with her fingers.

Wehrmacht guards stopped the vehicle and gave chase. The woman ran into her destroyed home to hide, but it was no use. The Nazis dragged her to the street where she was shot, her body dumped on the ground. The convoy went on.

DULAG LUFT

On June 30, Fall entered Dulag Luft, the Luftwaffe's infamous information center for Allied Air Force officers located near Frankfurt, Germany. Interrogators had learned physical violence was not the most effective means of obtaining information from prisoners.

POWs ('kriegies') walk the perimeter at Stalag Luft III.

Instead, they relied on mental depression, deprivation and psychological blackmail to break a prisoner's resolve.

An incoming prisoner would be placed in a solitary cell and threatened with starvation or death at the hands of the Gestapo. The prisoners received no cigarettes, toiletries, or Red Cross packages.

Fall was kept in his cell for seven days and nights. Each morning he scratched a notch in the wall with a fingernail to keep track of the days. His diet consisted of one slice of goon bread (nickname the prisoners gave bread served by German guards) and one cup of smelly water. Only one trip to the toilet was allowed per day.

Despite the deprivations, Fall continued to offer only name, rank, and serial number. Irritated with his non-cooperation, the Germans threw him into another filthy cell with a stench of excrement and vomit. When Fall dropped a wooden bunk, the room's only accommodation, dozens of fleas, ticks and lice emerged from the burlap mattress' wood shavings.

A heavily-barred window emitted a small amount of light. The huge door had a small peephole with pass-through flapper near the floor.

During the days and nights that followed, Fall heard sounds of torture, beatings and someone being sick outside. He found out years later they were recordings meant to intimidate.

At this time when his emotions threatened to uncoil and his sanity seemed fragile, Fall felt a hand on his shoulder. "You will be all right," a voice said. "It will not be easy but you will get back to your family and fiancé again."

Fall believed the words and presence at his side were from God. Though he had been raised attending church, he had fallen away in recent years. Now the touch on his shoulder and comforting words sustained him. He would continue

33

to rely on it through countless trials during the next several months.

STALAG LUFT III

On July 10, 1944, Fall and a handful of other POWs were transferred via train to Stalag Luft III near Zagan (then Sagan), Poland. In March 1944, the camp had gained notoriety when a massive escape by Allied service personnel via tunnels took place. The episode was portrayed in the 1963 movie 'The Great Escape' starring Steve McQueen.

The camp covered approximately 60 acres, much of it a pine forest over sandy soil. The camp was divided into compounds, each enclosed by two 12-foot barbed-wire fences. These fences ran parallel with six feet between them, the area inside filled with tangled barbed wire. About 25 feet inside the barrier running parallel with the fences was a small wire supported by stakes low to the ground. This was known as the 'Warning Wire.'

The camp with 12,000 POWs, mostly Americans, contained enlisted and officers, usually housed separately.

Within each barracks triple-deck bunks were arranged to form 12 room areas with a hallway down the middle. Each area was called a combine. Fourteen Allied prisoners were assigned to one combine. Each combine worked together as a family unit.

In an act of defiance the Allies called themselves 'kriegies' – an abbreviation of the German word for prisoner of war *"Kriegesgefangenen."* Each barracks with around 180 kriegies had a stove and limited coal ration. Each combine had a chief cook and kitchen patrol. These positions rotated among the members weekly. Combines adhered to strict use of the stoves.

Occasionally, the kriegies' inadequate diets were supplemented by packages from the Red Cross. A typical packet may contain a carton of K-2 biscuits, a carton of processed American cheese, bar of chocolate, soluble coffee, tin of corned beef, carton of dried prunes, liver paste, powdered milk, oleo, jam, pork luncheon meat, salmon, sugar, 100 cigarettes, soap and Vitamin C tablets. Each parcel was packed to provide proper nourishment for one man for a week.

Fall developed a high regard for the American Red Cross. "If it were not for the food parcels and medical supplies the Red Cross got to the POW camps, I would not have survived," he said.

Twice daily, no matter the weather, prisoners fell out to the parade ground for a head count. Lined up by blocks (a block was one end of a barracks) in military formation, they stood in straight rows side-by-side, five men deep. If contraband was suspected throughout the camp, the number of searches increased.

Soldiers on both sides of the war were captured as evidenced in this photo of a large number of German prisoners around Aachen, Germany, October 1944. National Archives

When the prisoners performed calisthenics, Fall, who had never received official medical treatment for his broken leg, could not comply.

A kriegie who had been a college medical student before the war requested medical supplies from the guards to put Fall's leg in a cast. All of the kriegies were shocked when the request was granted. With no other medical attention Fall's leg healed correctly for which he was immensely thankful.

Long days stretched before the prisoners. Some read books donated by the Red Cross and other groups. Some walked the perimeter of the camp. "I was known as a 'sack hound' because I slept so often," said Fall.

Fall wrote many letters to his family. It was a challenge to think of positive things to share which might relieve their minds about his welfare.

He couldn't tell them about the horror of bailing out of the flaming Thunderbolt, nor about the strafing with the German convoy. He didn't mention the suffering of the badly wounded Allied soldiers stuck in the garret in Chartres or the murder of the elderly woman outside her house of rubble.

He veered away from talk about his hunger, inability to get warm or need for medical attention, the dirty, crowded conditions, guard towers with searchlights and machine guns, crowded conditions and general grime he and the other POWs lived in.

In one letter Fall wrote:

Dear All:

I've finally reached a permanent prison camp. You can write to me here if you like but I expect to leave here before your letters have time to arrive. The broken leg I received in bailing out is healing nicely. I expect to take the cast off this week or next. Don't worry about me. The Red Cross has helped us a lot. We have a nice library. We have a school system with a number of classes. I've started Spanish. A large sports program with baseball, basketball, etc. is going on.

In addition to German rations, we have Red Cross parcels. We are divided into groups and do our own cooking. It is surprising what the fellows can do with a little bit of nothing.

As I've said before, don't worry about me for compared to what I've seen, this place is pretty nice. Like anything else, it is just what you make it. I'm lucky to be alive and spirited by dreams of the future, can endure this for the duration.

Love, Jim

He was discouraged to never receive letters from home. All incoming mail was censored and he suspected the Germans didn't pass his on.

When Fall felt he would go crazy with captivity, he focused on his family and Ethel Mae. His memories of these warm, loving people gave him strength and courage to face adversity while providing a reason to live.

During weeks leading up to Christmas, the kriegies saved a portion of their meager rations to celebrate the holiday. That night the Germans showed unexpected generosity by waiving early lockup so the kriegies could go from block to block seeing how other POWs had decorated.

In January 1945 Fall and the other prisoners heard guns and bombs outside the perimeter of the camp. They guessed it was the Russian military advancing westward, ready for vengeance.

German guards at Stalag Luft III grew increasingly nervous. On January 29, they ordered Fall's compound to pack their belongings.

For most men this consisted of nothing more than a bedroll, POW-issued top coats and sock caps. The men, many of whom were ill from the record-cold winter, proceeded to trudge toward Spremberg, Germany, a 65-mile journey in blizzard conditions.

Thoughts of family and fiancé Ethel Mae Swank buoyed Fall's spirits as a POW.

It was a trying time. One kriegie implored Fall's help with another prisoner whose feet were in bad shape. Fall put the sick man's arm on his shoulder and together he and the other kriegie carried, dragged and cajoled the injured soldier into walking the rest of the journey. Often, the sick man begged to be left behind. Fall and the other soldier refused.

Miraculously, every POW from Stalag Luft III survived the grueling trek.

At Spremberg the prisoners were packed into boxcars so tightly they couldn't all lay down. For three days and nights they had no food, water or toilet facilities. Many of the men developed dysentery and diarrhea. The stench of unwashed bodies, vomit and excrement was dehumanizing to Fall.

On February 7, the prisoners arrived, exhausted and in poor health, at Stalag VII-A near Moosburg, Germany. It was the largest German POW camp with approximately 110,000 prisoners. At one time during the war, men from every nation fighting against Germany were held there.

The weather at Moosberg was cold, damp and gloomy. On rare occasions when the sun appeared, men hung out their bedding. Bugs crawled out, attracted to the heat and the kriegies picked them off. At this camp no cooking stations were available, forcing the men to make their own stoves from empty food cans.

Despite the miserable conditions, Fall and the other men endured their captivity with hope as rumors of American troops in the area gradually leaked through.

Then on April 29, 1945, it happened.

A P-51 circled the camp at low altitude. When the plane turned to make a final pass, performing a roll, small arms fire, machine guns and mortars erupted from outside the camp. A group of P-47s and P-51s attacked targets in the area. When the men inside the barbed wire spied the lead tank of the 14th Armored Division lumbering over the horizon, they cheered wildly. Dozens of tanks charged through the fences into the former prison compound.

The jubilation of the liberated men was especially spirited when the hated Nazi swastika flag was ripped down to be replaced by a large, star-spangled American flag. "Every man had tears in his eyes," said Fall.

Ten months after his plane had been shot down, he was finally going home! He had turned 22 years old two days prior, but he would always count this day as his best present.

An Allied mobile bakery operated 24 hours a day, providing baked goods for the hungry men. Red Cross parcels, discovered in hiding places of the guards, were distributed and more trucked in from Switzerland.

General George S. Patton arrived on May 1. As a commander who took great pride in his troops, Patton reminded the flea-bitten men who had not had a bath, clean clothing or medical attention for months that they were soldiers of the United States. He encouraged them to shape up and look and act like soldiers.

Rather than hearing the speech as critical of their appearance, Fall was inspired by the general's words. "He wanted us to recall the pride and self-worth we had as soldiers," he said. The general's words continued to echo

General George S. Patton was a controversial Allied leader who led his troops to victory during the war.

through Fall's mind as he and the others left behind forever Stalag VII-A on the first leg of their long journey home.

The liberated men were flown to Camp Lucky Strike near LeHavre, France, where they received medical treatment, hot showers, and delousing and new uniforms. They were put on double hospital rations. During a physical exam, Fall discovered his weight had dropped 80 pounds.

After several days, the ex-POWs boarded ships for the United States. Fall learned that a few days after he was shot down, the 366th Fighter Group had moved to France, making it the first Allied Air Group to operate from French soil.

Back in Indiana, Fall was reunited with his family. They had received two telegrams about him from the United States government. The first on June 28, 1944, stated he was declared missing in action. On July 27, Fall's status of prisoner of war was confirmed with a second telegram.

Among personal effects sent home from Thruxton included a photo of Fall's sisters, Carol and June, in his wallet.

James Fall and Ethel Mae Swank were married on June 28, 1945, a year to the day his parents received the missing-in-action telegram. The couple would become parents to three children.

On November 15, 1945, Fall was promoted to First Lieutenant. On December 16, 1945, he was discharged from military service.

Using the GI Bill, Fall earned a Doctor of Dental Surgery degree at Indiana University. He worked as a dentist in Marion, Indiana, until retiring in 2001.

"It was a great honor to have engaged in combat in defense of one's country," he said. "My service ratings attest to my proficiency and dedication as a pilot. I am very proud that regardless of circumstances I served my country with pride, dignity and honor. During those woeful days of my imprisonment, I felt the hand of the Lord as He spoke to me. He did not forsake me."

Jack Humbrecht – Army Air Corps

'Achtung' was on fire!

On August 27, 1944, Second Lieutenant Jack Humbrecht and his B-17 crew of 10 were on their third bombing mission over German-occupied Europe when flames from anti-aircraft fire swiped the plane the crew had named 'Achtung'.

Humbrecht quickly ordered the crew to bail. Waiting until all had exited the plane, Humbrecht then jumped with his chute.

Exiting a plane in such a fashion was no guarantee of safety. Humbrecht was thankful to land without injury. He would be saddened to discover later three of his crew members had died from their falls. "They were good men," he said.

Humbrecht had no time to grieve as, upon landing, German civilians at gunpoint apprehended him. They locked him and other captured Allied flight crew members in an unheated barn. The next day, the group boarded a crowded train and taken to Stalag Luft III near the town of Sagan in Poland, 100 miles southeast of Berlin.

Stalag Luft III was established in March 1942 as a prisoner of war camp for Allied flight crews, including British and other Commonwealth officers.

Humbrecht had wanted to fly from the time he graduated from North Side High School in Fort Wayne, Indiana, in 1941. Thinking he would soon be drafted, Humbrecht enlisted in the Army Air Corps. At flight school in Columbus, Ohio, he learned to fly a Taylor Cub and B-17.

Humbrecht was thrilled to earn his wings and be assigned a 10-man B-17 crew with the 8th Air Force. The crew consisted of co-pilot, navigator, bombardier, engineer/ top turret gunner, radio operator, ball turret gunner, two waist gunners, and tail gunner.

Humbrecht's crew flew to Toronto, then on to the Azores Islands in Portugal before being assigned bombing missions in Africa. German General Erwin Rommel had control of eastern Africa. American forces flew low, whipping up sand to damage enemy tanks.

Humbrecht and his crew were only in Africa a short while before heading to northern Germany for bombing missions. His capture meant his assigned missions were over.

As the war progressed, the 60-acre camp of Stalag Luft III would grow to hold 2,500 Royal Air Force, 7,500 U.S. Army Air Force, and 900 officers from other Allied air forces.

The Germans ensured prisoners did not escape from Stalag Luft III by a number of methods. They enforced multiple daily roll calls. Prisoners received small portions of food. The only fare Humbrecht later remembered eating was kohlrabi.

During the war, 27,000 air crew members were shot down and captured by the Germans.

Guard dogs intimidated prisoners. If a prisoner moved during roll call, the canines snarled or bit them. Inside the barracks prisoners climbed three tiers of bunk beds to get away from the enraged beasts.

In retaliation the prisoners, who referred to themselves as *kriegies*, devised ways of countering the intimidation tactics. One was to call 'Tally Ho!' when a guard was near.

Despite the obstacles, Humbrecht and other prisoners never stopped looking for ways to escape. The most obvious was to dig escape routes. Some prisoners hid dirt inside their clothing until guards caught on and punished them.

Humbrecht wrote a letter to his family on forms supplied by his German guards.

One failed attempted mass escape from the north compound of Stalag Luft III had taken place in March 1944. Of 76 men who crawled to freedom, 73 were captured. Fifty were executed. The rest were returned to Stalag III or other camps where they remained through the end of the war.

Life in the POW camp was made slightly easier with the delivery of Red Cross packages and letters from home. On rare occasions the prisoners were offered the opportunity to write to their families and friends. Humbrecht used the German-issued stationery to pen this missive:

Jan. 8, 1945

Dear Mom & Dad

Here is a new year. The holidays have passed and although I wished I was at home, I can't complain about my Xmas & New Years. I also had a nice birthday. Morrie Butler baked me a cake and put happy birthday on it. It was all a surprise.

It sort of looks like I'll be here for a while yet so I'll make some parcel requests. When you send tobacco parcels, send me Model pipe tobacco and cigars. In my food parcels send me some socks, a pair of green pants and a green shirt. Also put a good pipe in each one. My pants size 32-32. A 15 ½-33 shirt.

I haven't received any word from you as yet. By the time you receive this both of you will have had a birthday. I hope they were happy ones. I suppose you both celebrated them. ha. I am studying German (not much success) and reviewing my high school algebra. Tell everyone I said hello.

The studying he referred to was organized by the prisoners to help pass the time. Humbrecht created a routine to keep his spirits positive. "Every day I told myself I would get out of there the next day," he said.

By spring 1945, the tide of the war had turned in favor of the Allies. This angered Nazi officials who ordered the kriegies to be loaded into '40-by-8' box cars – so named because during WWI they had been used to haul 40 soldiers or eight horses.

While enroute to another prison camp, the train was strafed by American P-51s. The Germans parked the cars between mountains, thus preventing the pilots from flying low enough to cause damage.

The diversion was enough for Humbrecht and two other POWs, both Americans, to sneak away. Despite their weakened conditions, the trio made it to a wood where they hid for several days.

The escapees eventually reached Russian territory where they were rescued and taken to Camp Lucky Strike at Le Havre, France, a place of departure for the Allies. At his physical examination Jack Humbrecht discovered he had lost 40 pounds in eight months of captivity.

Jack Humbrecht was awarded a Purple Heart. After his discharge in 1945, he married his high school sweetheart, Lauana Halter. They became the parents to two sons.

In Fort Wayne Jack co-owned a tavern, Jack and Johnny's, before retiring in the 1990s.

"Our flight crew did the best we could while flying bombing missions over German-occupied territory," he said.

William Ingram – Navy

"Abandon ship!"

William ('Bill') Ingram was below deck on the USS *Houston* when the ominous order was issued.

On February 28, 1942, the crew had become embroiled in yet another battle with the Japanese in the Java Sea. It was gritty and Ingram, a 17-year-old from Springfield, Illinois, tried to keep up with the rest of the crew's actions while at general quarters.

Ingram was assigned duties of a powder monkey. This meant shoving powder bags loaded in two-and-a-half-foot projectiles up an elevator from the depths of the ship to a gun crew in the turret on deck.

The powder bags for the ship's nine eight-inch guns could travel as far as 12 miles.

The Battle of the Java Sea was not the first time the crew of the *Houston* had nearly entered Davy Jones' Locker. The entire time Ingram had been on board the crew was at general quarters (battle stations). Ingram, youngest member of the 1,100-member crew, stayed in the turret so much that he never located his assigned bunk and locker. He slept under the turret and left the turret only to use the head (bathroom).

Recently, the Japanese had reported the *Houston* as sunk. The mighty vessel *had*, in fact, evaded so many attacks that she was given the name, "The Galloping Ghost of the Java Coast."

Bill Ingram joined the Navy to serve with his brother. His position afforded him a steady paycheck, place to sleep and chance to see the world.

At hearing the ship's captain order the crew to abandon ship, one part of Ingram's brain registered the words. If the ship was sinking, he needed to act fast -- either jump overboard or risk going down with the ship. Another part of his brain caused him to freeze in fear.

Born in 1924, Ingram had, like most Americans of the 1930s, learned to get along with little. He, his parents and three siblings had done without everything but necessities during the Great Depression. When his family's finances became severely strapped, Ingram quit school in the eighth grade to sell newspapers and work at a roller rink.

After his older brother, Robert, joined the United States Navy, Bill felt the same urge to go to sea. His goal was to serve on the same ship as Robert had been assigned -- the *Houston*.

In June 1941 his father William Ingram, Sr. signed a form, giving permission for Bill to enlist. Being in the Navy guaranteed a steady paycheck and 'three squares and a cot' -- military slang for three meals and a place to sleep, which were precious commodities at that time. He would also have the thrill of adventure in traveling around the world.

Bill Ingram traveled to Great Lakes Naval Training Center near Chicago for basic training. After graduating, he was overjoyed to receive his requested assignment for the *Houston*. But when he arrived at Hawaii in fall 1941, he discovered the *Houston* was at sea on maneuvers. He waited on the USS *Shalmat*, an old troop transport.

The *Shalmat* was five miles from Pearl Harbor on December 7, 1941, when Japanese planes attacked the

American Navy base. During the next couple of weeks, confusion reigned as the American military, disorganized and small in number, established itself to fight in two oceans.

At Christmas Bill Ingram had sailed with the USS *Pensacola* to Perth, Australia to help protect the country from an invasion. When granted shore leave, Ingram spent the holiday with a gracious Australian host family.

After the New Year, he boarded the *Houston* at Port Darwin. But by then, Robert had been re-assigned. Bill Ingram didn't mind as he daily learned about life at sea from older crew members.

Ingram was proud to be a member of the *Houston*, which was President Franklin D. Roosevelt's flagship – it was the ship the American leader traveled on.

Still, "Abandon ship!" were words every sailor dreaded to hear from his captain. Maybe this time the Galloping Ghost of the Java Coast had reached her end.

Ingram stood as dozens of members of the *Houston*'s crew rushed around him securing their safety. The teen seemed unable to think, too terrified to move.

Another sailor named Red Clymer, paused when he spotted the younger man. Ingram's haunted expression pulled at Clymer and he hauled Ingram to the side of the ship, trying to push the younger man over in an attempt to save his life. Ingram resisted, pulling back with unusual strength.

Clymer found a life ring for Ingram and flotation device for himself. The action of putting on the preserver seemed to establish a sense of calm over Ingram who allowed Clymer to shove his body over the bow before following.

USS *Houston* was known as 'The Gray Ghost of the Java Coast' for her evasive techniques.

The pair was instantly engulfed in a deluge of fuel oil and salt water. Dozens of heads bobbed in the water, as sailors fought to remain upright. The sea which they had gazed at for months with camaraderie and respect now became traitorous as a deadly arena.

Clymer shouted at Ingram to swim away from the ship as fast as possible. Ingram nodded. He knew when the *Houston* rolled, its back tow would pull anyone under who was close.

Ingram shot through the water as fast as his skinny arms would take him. Oil caked his face, making it difficult to see. With a thankful heart he recalled the instructor who had given him free swimming lessons during childhood at the local YMCA.

The night's only illumination was lights from the burning, sinking ship. Drowning bodies lay scattered as men submitted to a watery grave. For several minutes Ingram used every ounce of strength to propel himself through the water, even as his limbs grew heavy as lead.

After plowing through the tumultuous waves for a long while, Ingram paused to gulp in deep breaths. Twisting his body to check on the progress of Clymer, he panicked at not spying the sailor. Ingram called out for Clymer, but the sound dissipated among the other bodies screaming frantically for help.

Feeling very alone, Ingram resumed swimming while praying for Clymer's safety.

The terrifying night passed slowly with Ingram treading water in the cold sea. Eventually, a Japanese patrol boat spied him. The enemy! Ingram knew he would soon drown from exhaustion. He had no choice but to go aboard the vessel.

Barefoot and dressed only in underwear, he was interrogated by Japanese guards:

"What was your captain's name on the Houston?"

"Who is greater, Roosevelt or Tojo?"

Although Ingram had been on the *Houston* for two months, in his fright and exhaustion he couldn't recall the captain's name. He didn't recognize the name Tojo (the Japanese emperor), but knew the American president.

When he answered "Roosevelt", his ignorance cost him a beating.

Disgusted with their inadequate captive, the guards threw Ingram overboard. As soon as his body hit the water, Ingram dived to dodge Japanese bullets pinging off the surface as enemy sailors shot at him. Staying underwater until his lungs felt like bursting, he swam as far as possible before quietly going to the top for air.

His efforts helped him escape detection and Ingram felt relief to be reunited in the water with other survivors of the *Houston*. One sailor's face and an ear had been horribly burned. Ingram traded his life ring for the injured sailor's life jacket, though the latter was full of water.

The group bobbed several hours until a native fishing boat approached. When the owner demanded payment for space in his boat, those in the water with something to offer were picked up. Ingram despaired. With only his shorts, belt and a knife, he had nothing to barter. However, the fisherman liked the knife and pulled Ingram aboard.

After the fisherman had turned away several sailors, those in the boat grew disgusted with his greed and threw him overboard before hauling in the rejected men. The vessel sailed toward the beach where Ingram and the rest hoped to find help among the Dutch people of Java.

After docking, they walked until spotting a building with a red cross on the front. It appeared to be a former prison. Cautiously, they approached. When the people inside seemed eager to offer food and clothing, the Americans gratefully ate a meal and bedded down in the cells. Upon awaking, however, they found the cells locked. It had been a trap. The Javanese men in charge of the prison notified Japanese officials in the area and Ingram again became a captive of the Japanese.

The prisoners were taken to a theater in Serang, Java, where they were tied together in pairs. After several weeks, they traveled to a place in Batavia called Bicycle Camp, appropriately named because everyone rode the human-powered, two-wheeled vehicles.

Food for the prisoners consisted of small portions of rice balls. To appease their extreme hunger, the prisoners ate birds, lizards, bugs, worms -- whatever they could find. "If a snake was found, we'd kill it, cook it and chop it into sections to share," said Ingram. "It was eat to live."

American POWs celebrate July 4, 1942 in a Japanese prison camp. Such a celebration was against Japanese regulations. Discovery could have meant death. National Archives

Due to his small size, Ingram was assigned the task of scurrying up coconut trees for fruit.

During a transfer to Singapore, the prisoners met a group of Allied POWs who shared clothing with them. They were then loaded onto a ship with little drinking water and no private toilets, sailing to Moulmein, Burma. After marching barefoot for miles, they arrived at a place where the Japanese were building a railroad.

Plans for the Thai-Burma railroad were for it to stretch 250 miles to Bangkok. Its purpose was to transport Japanese troops and weapons in the Burma campaign of the war.

Work on the railroad was done with the labor of 250,000 prisoners, including American, British, Australian and Burmese. Korean nationals, also POWs, served as guards.

Each prisoner worked 12 hours a day, digging to remove a meter of dirt (two buckets). They worked to meet the quota during the monsoon season and in hot, dry weather.

Prisoners were not allowed to talk or communicate with each other while at their tasks. If guards thought a prisoner was not putting forth enough effort, the beat the prisoner with bamboo poles, pickaxes or rifles. When a prisoner fell in exhaustion, he was beaten often to death.

Of the approximately 102,000 Allied prisoners who died, most were buried close to the railroad. Due to the brutal working conditions, the project became known as the "Railway of Death."

A Dutch doctor named Hekking attempted to treat sick prisoners. As a POW, he was given few supplies, mostly bandages and quinine pills. Hekking relied heavily on herbs from the jungle. "All of the medicine he had could fill a baseball cap," said Ingram.

The prisoners were bordered by jungle and guards with no fences or gates. But overworked and underfed, they had no desire to run.

Ingram witnessed three men shot for trying to escape. Though discouraged, he kept his spirits revived by promising himself that rescue would happen next week.

In June 1945 Ingram contracted dysentery and malaria. The severity of the diseases caused him to suffer long periods of delirium.

Once, Ingram saw his body lying in an open area. When a plane flew low and strafed the area, Ingram screamed, knowing he was exposed with no protection.

Another time he awoke suddenly to see he appeared to be lying on a litter in a warehouse. Trying to ask those around him how long he had been unconscious was futile -- no one could hear him.

Each time Ingram awakened as if from a deep sleep. He always seemed to be in a new place. He finally gave up, believing he was dead and floating in heaven.

At one point a movement awoke him. When Ingram looked around, he saw he was being loaded on a litter in to a plane. Panicking, he thrashed about. Was the enemy sending him to yet another miserable camp?

Gentle hands pushed him back to the stretcher. It occurred to Ingram he was being cared for. Despite his weak state, he felt stronger than in a long time. Was the war over? Exhausted, he fell asleep.

The war had ended. Ingram's body had been retrieved from the prisoner of war camp and he was flown to a hospital in New York City where he received weeks of medical care.

After he had recovered, the military issued Ingram and other liberated soldiers new uniforms and some cash. The liberated men planned to celebrate.

As Ingram was 20 years old, he was still too young to buy an alcoholic drink. Instead, the soldier who had spent three years as a prisoner of war ordered a head of lettuce. "It tasted great!" he said.

Anxious to get home, Ingram hopped on a troop train to Illinois. He didn't notify his family, which he later regretted as his mother nearly had a heart attack at finding him on her doorstep.

During their joyful reunion, his family told him they had received three cards from him during his time as a POW. He didn't recall sending them and guessed they were propaganda mailers sent by the Japanese, stating he was being treated well.

Coincidentally, his brother Robert had also been captured at Corregidor in the Philippines. The family had received similar cards from him. The two brothers were reunited two weeks later when Robert arrived home, frail and emaciated but alive.

Bill Ingram stayed in the Navy for 22 years, retiring at the rank of Chief Petty Officer. He later worked in the iron industry and lived with his wife and two children in Jacksonville, Florida.

Allied prisoners of war at a prison camp near Yokohama cheer and wave flags upon being rescued, August 1945. National Archives

Over the next several decades, Hollywood made several movies about POWs and their experiences. Bill Ingram condemned the 1957 Hollywood film, '*Bridge on the River Kwai*'. "It depicted prisoners getting along with their Japanese captors," he said. "It didn't happen that way." He recommended the 2001 movie '*To End All Wars*', starring Robert Carlyle, as better reflecting the true nature of the experiences.

Ingram attributed his survival as a prisoner of war to his upbringing. "I grew up poor so I was used to eating few meals and having no luxuries," he said. "I loved being in the military and would do it again except for the Burmese part."

Note: Of the 1,068 men who manned the *Houston*, approximately 368 escaped from the sinking ship. Most were captured in the sea or jungles of Java. Only 289 survived in Japanese prisoner of war camps.

The Thai portion of the railway continues to exist. Out of respect for the dead soldiers that built the Kwai Bridge, a new bridge was built and the original bridge closed to trains in 2014. The bridge is still open to foot traffic.

Walter Rumple – Army Air Corps

A single dim light illuminated the hold of the ship where 1,800 men stood crushed together. A few among the tired bodies raised their heads, desperately gasping for a breath of fresh air of which there was none in the fetid compartment. The only good thing about being packed tightly was they could hold each other up, while allowing some prisoners a chance to sit.

As the Russian army had begun making their way west in the latter part of World War II, German guards and officials at Stalag VI, a prisoner of war camp in the northernmost confines of the German Reich (what is today Lithuania), had received orders to move their prisoners.

In early 1945, the large group of weak and often ill men had boarded a decrepit sea craft at the port of Memel on the Baltic coast. During the sea journey which took days, the prisoners suffered dehydration, starvation, and dysentery.

No toilet was available. The only way for the men to dispose of bodily wastes was a bucket. Each day it was lowered into the hold. When filled with human waste, the bucket was retrieved. That same bucket also held the men's drinking water. Each day the dehydrated men greedily gulped to quench their aching thirsts, too sick and tired to care about germs.

As the miserable journey continued, some men began to fret about its destination. For 18-year-old Walter Rumple, radio operator on a B-17, it didn't matter where the ship docked. He was determined to survive any hell the Germans put him through.

Walter Rumple served as a radio operator in B-17s in the Army Air Corps.

Rumple was born in 1925 in the town of Van Buren, Indiana, population 900. He was the youngest of seven children born to William and Florence Rumple. William supported his family by building bridges for the state highway department.

Walter, also called Bud, was a good student at Van Buren High School. He earned money after school by working at a local restaurant and delivering milk with his brother.

The life of the Rumple family changed, as it did for nearly every American family, on December 7, 1941. Shortly after the Japanese attack of naval forces on Pearl Harbor, Congress declared war on the Axis Powers and many American men hurried to join the military to defend their country.

Seventeen-year-old Bud Rumple, too young to enlist, anxiously watched as three of his brothers became part of various branches of the military.

A few months passed. Bud's desire to do something for his country caused him to take drastic actions. He quit school. Then he altered the date of birth on his birth certificate to show he was 18 years old and old enough to enlist in the Army Air Corps. "It felt like serving my country was something I should do," he said.

The Army Air Corps was the newest branch of the military. Flight crew members were needed to fill slots. When accepted for a bomber squadron, Rumple was thrilled. He didn't care what aircraft he flew in, he just wanted to beat the Nazis from the air.

After passing a physical exam at Fort Benjamin Harrison in Indianapolis, Rumple completed basic training at

Atlantic City, New Jersey. The recruits marching drills on the boardwalk.

Rumple spent six months at radio operator and flight mechanic school in Sioux Falls, South Dakota, and four months at aerial gunnery school in the Las Vegas desert. It was his first time to fly and he loved it.

In June 1942 Rumple was assigned to a B-17 crew with the 305th Bombardment Group of the Eighth Air Force. The B-17 was developed by the Boeing Company in the 1930s. Approximately 12,700 B-17s would be built between 1936 and 1945. With four-engines and multiple machine gun emplacements the aircraft received a nickname: 'Flying Fortress.'

The B-17s saw action in the European and Pacific Theaters of Operation during the war and would drop more bombs than any other American aircraft.

A B-17 crew consisted of four officers (pilot, co-pilot, navigator, bombardier) and six enlisted men (flight engineer, radio operator, two waist gunners, ball turret gunner positioned under the plane and tail gunner).

Rumple, youngest member of the crew, served as radio operator out of the radio room behind the bomb bays. He and the gunners operated 50-caliber machine guns.

The 305th had their primary training base at Geiger Field in Spokane, Washington. Crews completed six weeks of advanced flight training, practicing enemy maneuvers using AT-6's, nicknamed 'Texans'. The AT-6's were two-place planes with a pilot and gunner. A second plane pulled a target at which the gunner fired live tracer bullets to learn how to shoot at moving objects. "I always felt compassion for the pilot of those tow planes because some of our bullets went astray," said Rumple.

In Lincoln, Nebraska, Rumple's crew received a new B-17 which they excitedly practiced maneuvers with. It was at this locale that Sergeant Rumple ran into some trouble – not in the air but on the ground. And not with the enemy but his own crew members.

Rumple was with his them at a roadhouse when his co-pilot asked Rumple to accompany him to their hotel. Rumple agreed. As it was raining, the bombardier, who was also at the roadhouse, offered his lieutenant's top coat and cap to Rumple. Rumple appreciated the officer's offer and left, wearing the garment with bars on his shoulders.

When the two men arrived at the hotel, the co-pilot retrieved something from his room. Bud waited in the lobby. The crew's pilot spotted Rumple in the lobby wearing the coat and cap. He berated Rumple for attempting to impersonate an officer. Such an action was against military protocol.

Rumple tried to explain the situation, as did the co-pilot who re-entered the room in time to hear the reprimand. The pilot refused to listen and told Rumple he would talk to him further about the matter the next morning.

Before the two could converse, the base commander who had overheard the conversation in the hotel spoke to

Rumple, saying he could not allow the incident to pass. Rumple would be demoted from the rank of sergeant to private.

Though originally upset, the pilot assured Rumple his rank of sergeant would be restored once the crew arrived in England. The pilot carried through with his promise.

Rumple's days of shenanigans were not over. As the plane's radio operator, he received briefings for bad weather during flights which he passed on to the pilot. If weather was bad before the plane approached the Great Lakes, the crew was to return to their base in Lincoln. Upon encountering bad weather after crossing the Great Lakes, they were to land at Baer Field at Fort Wayne,

Walter Rumple (standing, second from left) served with a crew of the 305th Bombardment Group of the Eighth Air Force.

69

Indiana. Baer Field was only 45 minutes from Rumple's hometown of Van Buren.

On one occasion, he received information about upcoming turbulence. Rumple disconnected the wires on his radio until the plane had crossed the Great Lakes. Then he reconnected and informed the pilot of the approaching bad weather. The plane landed at Baer Field where the crew waited five days for the skies to clear. This gave Rumple a chance to visit with friends and family. It was his only time to do so during the war.

In fall 1942 Rumple's crew received orders to head to the British Isles. They flew the North Atlantic route from Maine-Gander, Newfoundland to Belfast, Ireland. In December the group arrived at Chelveston, England where the 305th bomb group was based.

The Americans flew during the day while the British flew at night. Altitudes of 20,000 feet and higher caused the temperature inside the plane to plummet as low as negative 40 degrees. To avoid frostbite the men wore heated flight suits and boots.

Each mission had a designated target, usually oil refineries, ball bearing plants, or railroads. To defend their homeland the Nazis sent up flak (anti-aircraft fire) from anti-aircraft guns. The Allies also were attacked from German Luftwaffe (Air Force) fighters -- Fulk Wolf 90s, Messerschmidts 109s, JU 88s Junkers.

Rumple's crew knew they were a replacement crew. During the war, the 305th flew 337 missions, while suffering tragic losses of 154 aircraft with 10 members per crew.

Anti-aircraft fire was especially heavy in the German cities of Schweinfurt, Osburg, Leipzig, Wilhelmshaven, and Frankfurt. Among Rumple's crew's first eight missions, three were over Frankfurt.

SHOT DOWN

On March 2, 1944, Rumple's crew prepared for their ninth mission, again over Frankfurt. Rising at 0400 hours they ate breakfast and were briefed on the mission, including the target.

While the crew was occupied, the plane's crew chief took time to paint a bomb on the side of the plane. He usually painted the symbol recognizing a completed mission upon the crew's return but had been too busy the day prior.

When he suggested painting a bomb for that day's mission, the crew objected. "We all agreed we should complete the mission first," said Rumple. As it happened, the crew chief would never paint that day's bomb.

The day started out well with the crew successfully dropping bombs on Frankfurt. As the plane turned westward toward the English Channel, it flew approximately two hours before encountering anti-aircraft fire.

When a ME-109 fired 20-mm shells, Rumple's pilot tried evasion tactics. Unfortunately, the number three engine caught fire, forcing the pilot to feather the prop and shut down the engine. The crew's efforts to maintain control of the plane failed. As the flames increased, the pilot could wait no longer – reluctantly he gave the order for the crew to bail out.

Hundreds of parachutes descend as paratroopers bail out of planes to land in Holland. September 1944. National Archives

The next few minutes seemed petrifying for the crew who had never practiced jumping from a plane. Rumple held his composure as he helped the ball turret gunner place Eddy Fernandez, waist gunner, into his chute. Fernandez's leg had been severely pierced by shrapnel and he was unconscious. Gripping Fernandez's hand around the rip cord of his chute, they pushed him out of the burning plane, praying the cold air would revive the injured man and his hand would jerk the chute open.

Then it was their turn to exit the plane.

A chute harness was designed to snap around the wearer's legs and chest. Rumple had found it uncomfortable to wear the tight leg straps during a flight and often left them unfastened.

Now, as he floated through the air, Rumple fought a growing sense of panic. His leg straps were not secured and he feared he would slide out of his harness.

He reached up to steer the chute's shroud lines for a safe landing. The maneuver worked and Rumple landed without mishap in a snow-covered field.

He quickly hid the chute, though its white silky fabric blended with the opaqueness of the two feet of snow on the ground. Rumple also stuffed his pistol under a nearby bush, afraid if he kept it, he'd be tempted to use it. He didn't want to die for trying to defend himself.

Then Rumple began running through an open field, the deep snow hampering his efforts. As he scanned the area for crew members, his hopes plummeted. None were visible. Rumple had no idea which direction to go.

At the sound of barking dogs behind him, Rumple slowed. The sight of German farmers emerging from a woods, carrying clubs, pitchforks and guns, brought him to a stop. Placing hands on his knees, he sucked in deep breaths, trying to slow his racing heart. Any hope of evading capture had burst like a stuck balloon.

One man pointed a gun in Rumple's direction, motioning for him to draw closer. Rumple obeyed, trembling with fear. Would the man shoot him and leave his body to the dogs?

He led Rumple to a farmhouse where five old ladies sat in the kitchen. The women tried to communicate with the young prisoner who understood nothing but the word 'Chicago.' When Walter asked in English for a drink of water, the women gave him a cup of weak coffee.

A German guard motioned for Rumple to walk outside. When the ladies began to cry, the teen feared for his life more than when he had been forced to bail from the burning plane.

The guard led Rumple to a barn. Inside, Rumple's spirits lifted as he spotted members of his crew locked in a make-shift cell. While sorry they had been captured, he was thrilled to be reunited.

Several Allied planes had been shot down in the area during the war and the villagers prepared the barn cell to hold captured crew members for the Nazis.

The next day Rumple and other American air crew members boarded a train for Dulag Luft, an interrogation center for Allied Air Force personnel near Frankfurt.

Upon arriving, the men were separated and asked a number of questions in English by a German commander:
- What bomb squadron had he been part of?
- Who was his base commander?

- Where had the flight crew been headed?

Rumple offered only name, rank, and serial number, as specified for prisoners of war by the Geneva Convention. For his succinct replies Rumple was put into solitary confinement for two days. Later, he was drilled again with the same questions.

Allied troops fight for freedom in many parts of Europe, April 1945. National Archives

On the German commander's desk Rumple spotted a newspaper covering a book. Noticing Rumple's attention, the commander moved the newspaper so the book underneath was revealed. It was for the 305th Bomb Group. Rumple's spine tingled as he realized the commander knew more details about his squadron than he had pretended.

STALAG LUFT VI

The rest of Rumple's crew were likewise drilled under threat of death to provide information to the Germans. When none was forthcoming, the Germans forced Rumple and the other POWs to board crowded train cars. They rode for two days to East Prussia near the Lithuanian border to Stalag Luft VI.

The POW camp had been built in 1939 to hold Allied Air Force personnel, including British, French, Belgian, Russian, Polish, Canadian and American. By July 1944, it would house 9,000 Allied airmen.

The location of the camp, set in a forest clearing one-and-a-half miles square, had been chosen because foliage and underbrush in the swampy area served as a barrier to escape attempts. Two fences ten feet high surrounded the camp with electrically-charged wires. Those formidable obstacles, combined with the camp's location near the icy Baltic Sea, made surviving as a prisoner a distinct challenge.

The POWs were assigned to the camp's 10 single-story brick barracks. Guards with machine guns and dogs trained to attack kept a close watch on activities from towers equipped with powerful spotlights. The men were told anyone caught attempting to escape would be shot.

Weeks, then months passed. The idea of trying to escape seemed overwhelming to the POWs, especially as they were kept weak from a lack of food. Thin potato soup, an occasional piece of cabbage, and bread made up their daily diet.

Bread, hauled in to the camp on a horse-drawn wagon, uncovered and stacked like firewood, lay exposed to weather, dust and insects. If the loaves tasted like sawdust, there was a good reason -- it was a principal ingredient.

RED CROSS
The Red Cross, an international relief agency, attempted to supplement the prisoners' diets with packages of food and blankets. Each man should have received one parcel per week. However, guards pilfered through the packages, taking what they wanted. A POW may only receive half a parcel every other week.

Before distributing the remainder of the Red Cross packages, guards opened everything, forcing the starving men to consume it all immediately. This prevented hoarding for escape attempts.

Sometimes the packages caused more dissention than aid. "We divided the packages amongst ourselves," said Rumple. "But we were so hungry that every guy thought his neighbor had a bigger portion than his own."

One of the most sought-after commodities from packages was cigarettes. They were a means of exchange, especially with guards.

News from the outside world was valuable to the prisoners. The primary source lay with the camp's hidden radio, created from random parts found throughout the camp. Assembled daily, it revealed much-desired news to the men about the war and elsewhere in the world from the British Broadcasting Corporation (BBC).

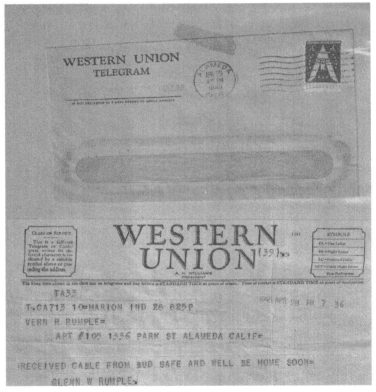

Members of Walter Rumple's family sent this telegram to other loved ones at exciting news of his release as a POW.

A POW chosen to be a runner listened to the broadcasts, then carried the information to each barracks. Each broadcast boosted the morale of the captured men. When not in use, the radio parts were hidden in various places in the camp.

The concealment was necessary as guards conducted barracks checks randomly. If some piece of contraband was suspected, the prisoners could stand for hours, often in cold weather.

In order to preserve structure inside the camp, one Allied man was voted by the others as their representative with the camp's commandant. Called 'The Confidence Man', he dealt directly with German officials on behalf of the POWs. "What he said went among us in the camp," said Rumple.

The Confidence Man determined use of the radio and the prisoners' reaction to news. This was especially true for D-Day. As the airmen learned of the Allies landing at Normandy, they wanted to cheer and shout.

However, the Confidence Man strictly warned them not to show any emotion that would tip off the guards about the source of information. Under threat that a search could reveal the radio, the prisoners maintained their composure while playing cards, walking around the fenced-in area and exercising. The radio was never found.

As the war continued, the men had to deal with the growing number of sicknesses in the camp, including dysentery – an infection thought to be spread through contaminated food or water. Symptoms include abdominal pain, cramps, and fever.

Living together under challenging circumstances drew the men together in camaraderie. When Rumple developed painful boils on his shoulder and back, making it hard to sleep, a POW named Riley (Rumple never learned the man's first name) cared for them.

The men also tried to help each other's mental health by encouraging them to refrain from using profanity. "Being able to rely on friends in the camp helped with our survival," said Rumple.

He remained positive about his chances of survival by thinking of all he had to go home to – family and friends, especially a young lady named Margaret Ballinger. She and Rumple had dated in high school. Margaret wrote to him often.

Rumple learned from letters from family that they had not been notified until April 1943 – a month after his capture – about his status of Missing in Action (MIA). Another four weeks passed before his family knew he was a POW. They had no idea of his location.

The POWs were allowed to write two letters each month on paper supplied by their captors. Rumple wrote home as often as he could.

He also turned to the one means of help that was readily available -- prayer. "I never thought much about prayer before I became a POW," he said. "When a person goes through something like that, you lean on it. I know prayer helped."

Newspaper reporters interview 'Tokyo Rose' -- Iva Toguri -- an American-born Japanese propagandist during the war, September 1945. National Archives.

In July 1944, information received indicated that Russian forces were drawing close to Stalag Luft VI. Orders were given for the POWs to be moved to another camp.

On July 13th, 1,800 men from Stalag Luft VI were taken to the port of Memel, a city in Lithuania on the Baltic coast. Forced aboard an unseaworthy ship, the men endured days of filth, lack of nourishment and fatigue. They could only hope their new destination would be an improvement on Stalag Luft VI.

It was worse.

The ship docked at Swinemunde, a city in northwest Poland on the Baltic Sea. Rumple and the others boarded a train with just as crowded and unsanitary conditions as the dilapidated ship. The only means of fresh air was a small window high on a wall.

On rare occasions when the train stopped after days of travel, guards opened the doors. It was not enough for several men who died.

STALAG IV

When the train's doors opened, the suffering men were greeted by soldiers who may have been Hitler Youth. Their young faces shone with glee as they lined the two-and-a-half mile road from the train station to the camp. Each one held a fixed bayonet.

The POWs, chained together, stumbled past the teens who exuberantly jabbed at them. A German captain riding on the running board of a vehicle shot his pistol in the air, while shouting words of encouragement to the young men. Angry dogs bit the prisoners' ankles.

Before leaving Stalag Luft VI, every POW had gathered his belongings, such as they were – perhaps a family photo, letters or a Bible. With no other means of control of their lives, the men hung on to the items as an act of defiance throughout their imprisonments.

During the run to Stalag Luft IV, however, most of the precious items were dropped and trod upon.

At one point Rumple was hit across his back with a rifle butt by a guard. "I felt lucky not to be bayoneted," he said.

The Commandant at Stalag Luft IV made no pretense of showing consideration for his prisoners. He allowed ill treatment by guards, especially one nicknamed Big Stoop by the inmates. Standing well over six feet, the guard walked with bent shoulders in a threatening manner amongst the prisoners. When provoked, which was often, his hands -- the size of dinner plates -- clapped prisoners open-palmed on the ears, painfully rupturing eardrums.

DEATH MARCH

The prisoners endured Stalag Luft IV through the long winter with record-low temperatures.

Following a dismal defeat at the Battle of the Bulge, Nazi troops recognized the war was nearly at an end. Still, they refused terms of an unconditional surrender as stipulated by the Allies.

When the commandant of Stalag Luft IV received orders to move the POWs to a different location where they would be hidden and unable to be liberated, he rounded them up and on February 6, the group walked out of the camp.

It was the toughest challenge yet for the POWs. They began the journey with two blankets and a top coat, which offered little protection, especially at night. The men gathered pine branches on which to sleep on top of the deep snow.

Field Marshall Wilhelm Keitel signs surrender terms for the German Army at Russian Headquarters in Berlin, May 7, 1945. National Archives.

For 55 days the men walked. And walked. Nearly 400 miles they traversed across mountains, back roads, forests and villages – often covering the same areas. It was obvious the Germans didn't know where to put the POWs. The pointless flight became known as a 'German Death March.'

When barns were available, German officers took refuge. Farmers refused entry to the prisoners. By now, most were sick and unable to control their bowels. Their only food was an occasional potato.

In early April, despite cold weather, ill health, snow and unfamiliarity with the area, Rumple and four men from his flight crew began to talk about escape.

Each day the guards gave the prisoners 10-minute rests in the morning and afternoon. When the whistle blew to assemble, it took several minutes for the huge group of tired men to shuffle to their feet and form lines.

An area with brush for cover could provide the opportunity for Rumple and the others to get away. They had no way of knowing where the front lines were, but the men figured they had nothing to lose. They would search for leftover potatoes, carrots, and cabbage in fields.

The plan happened the way they hoped. One day, when the guards blew their whistles, Rumple and his group sprinted toward a woods. The guards fired a few shots, but no pursuit ensued. Everyone knew the war was over in everything but name. Perhaps the German guards figured they should treat the prisoners better as the situation might soon be reversed.

Rumple and his group ran for days. At one point they selected a base, hiding during the day, and venturing out at night to find the front lines, food and water.

One night they heard voices. Excited to think they were near freedom, the group drew closer. They were horrified to spy a German army camp a few yards away. Quickly they retreated to their base, trekking in a different direction the following night.

Upon finding a boat at a river, they were about to set out when they again spotted a German camp. By now, their bellies hurt from hunger. The Allies returned to their hiding place, wondering if their run for freedom was in vain.

On the morning of April 18, 1945, the men awoke to the sound of small arms fire. Branches above their heads dropped snow due to the concussion of guns and tanks. The question was, who did the artillery belong to?

They had slept in a ravine. Rumple dug deeper in the ground. "Please God," he prayed, "let me live so I can marry Margaret."

The prisoners ran to the river. Though the water was freezing, they swam as fast as they could from the sound of the guns.

Dragging themselves from the water, the men hid alongside a road to see what vehicles would pass. The first vehicle looked promising -- it had Allied markings!

However, the next vehicle belonged to a German truck driver. Desperate with hunger, the POWs flagged him down, demanding to be taken to Allied lines.

The driver had received permission from the Allies to evacuate and was hauling items from his store in Hamburg to a new location. He agreed to take the men. They climbed in the back of his truck, uncertain if they would still be free at the end of the day.

The truck carried crates of canned food. Not knowing or caring what was inside, the men broke open the contents with pen knives found in another box. They gorged themselves, only feeling sick upon reading the labels – the cans contained horse meat.

The truck driver, true to his word, took the men to a British encampment. After more than a year in the hands of the German Army, Rumple and the others were finally free!

They boarded a troop ship to Belgium, along with other POWs who had escaped or been liberated. Rumple had lost approximately 30 pounds during his imprisonment.

The POWs were flown to London where they convalesced in a military hospital while submitting to intensive debriefings.

After many days, the men were pronounced healthy and received passes to see the huge, historical city. On May 5, 1945, Walter Rumple was standing in front of Buckingham Palace listening to victory speeches for Victory in Europe Day. People filled the streets, celebrating the war's end.

While happy the war was over, Rumple wanted nothing more than to be reunited with his family and Margaret.

On June 30, 1945, Rumple wedded Margaret Ballinger, a marriage that would last 70+ years.

Finally, in June Walter Rumple returned to the United States on the USS *John Ericsson*.

On June 30, 1945, he and Margaret Ballinger were united in marriage. He had received a 30-day leave and planned a honeymoon. When a military telegram arrived, Rumple despaired, believing it was an order for him to report to a base to be shipped overseas. Scuttlebutt said a major invasion of Japan was being planned to end the war.

His worries were for naught -- the typed message stated he had been granted another 30-day leave.

Walter Rumple was discharged a few months later. He and Margaret settled in southern Indiana where they raised five children.

All of Rumple's crew survived, but they never met together after the war, Rumple was contacted in later years by family members of the crew, asking information about their loved ones' military service which he gladly provided.

One of those family members was a grandson of Eddy Fernandez. In 2011 he phoned Rumple to say Eddy had survived his fall from the plane and spent time in a German hospital where doctors amputated his injured leg.

Fernandez was repatriated to the United States during a prisoner exchange. He died in 1989. The grandson ended the call by thanking Rumple for helping his grandfather escape.

For many years Rumple suffered from nightmares as a result of the war. He rarely spoke about his experiences as a POW. Then, as requests to share his stories occurred, he agreed to talk about it.

"It is hard to imagine humans treating each other that way," he told a school group. "So many people around the world don't have the freedoms we take for granted every day."

Rumple was not bitter about his time as a POW. "I have never regretted it," he said. "It was something that had to be done. We had been attacked. The American people pulled together and put an end to it. It was unbelievable how patriotic people were. They would do anything for our country. I'm still a softie when it comes to the American flag. It feels like seeing a lost brother. It bothers me when people disrespect our flag."

Rumple doesn't consider himself a hero. "The real heroes were the ones that never came back."

He acknowledges the power of prayers sent on his behalf by family and friends. "I think those prayers helped me survive," he said. "I knew people were praying and they made me a better person. Anyone who went through something like that is bound to be a better person, especially in faith. If your faith doesn't get stronger, there's something wrong."

Wilbert Seibold –

Army Air Corps

The two men slipped among the trees, running as fast as their exhausted, thin bodies could carry them. The crashing through snow-covered bare limbs sounded like a herd of elephants on a rampage to Staff Sergeant Wilbert Seibold. Yet no German shouts of alarm at discovering their escape reached the pair as they trudged deeper into the underbrush.

Wilbert 'Curly' Seibold (nicknamed for his wavy hair) and a fellow POW named Dean (Seibold didn't know his last name) had endured months of imprisonment in the German camp, Stalag Luft III, after their planes had been shot down over German-occupied territory. They had belonged to different flight crews but both were Americans.

In the early months of 1945, German guards had forced hundreds of emaciated, inadequately-dressed POWs to march in blizzard-like conditions, stopping only for breaks in the mornings and afternoons.

Seibold and Dean believed the regular breaks could work in their favor. The time it took for the exhausted Allied air crew members to rise to their feet, get in lines and resume marching was considerable. Hopefully, in the confusion the guards would not notice them slip away.

When his crew was shot down over German-occupied Europe, Curly Seibold (front row, far right) was captured. He refused to accept the life of a POW, attempting four times to escape.

The pair knew the key to a successful escape was showing no excitement or tension. Still, when the keening of the guard's whistle hit the air, Seibold had to fight his body's reaction to jump with anticipation.

Slowly, the two edged away from the group. Their plan seemed to work as all of the guards' backs were turned at the same time. Renewed strength flowed through their weak bodies as they stumbled into the nearby woods.

This was not Seibold's first attempt at escape. He had tried twice before during the incredibly cold winter at Stalag Luft III but was caught each time. He was determined to make this attempt count.

Wilbert Seibold was born in Zanesville, Indiana in 1923. He grew up on a farm with his parents, Charles and Edith, and sister Betty. After graduating from Lafayette Center High School in Allen County in 1941, he worked for a year before being drafted into the U.S. Army.

Seibold had known a pair of brothers who had been assigned as pilot and navigator with the Army Air Corps, the military's newest branch. Believing that serving as part of a flight crew sounded exciting, Seibold applied to be assigned to the Army Air Corps.

At that time openings in the Army Air Corps were available and Seibold was accepted as a gunner on a B-17 bomber. After completing basic training at Camp Perry in Ohio, he spent months at various bases learning skills as a radio operator and gunner: St. Petersburg, Florida; Las Vegas; Ardmore, Oklahoma; Kearney, Nebraska.

At Camp Kilmore, New Jersey, gunners practiced with 50-caliber ammunition on B-17s, using different colors to see who hit targets and who needed additional practice.

Seibold attended radio school at Sioux Falls, South Dakota. At Salt Lake City he met his 10-member flight crew who was assigned to the 331st squadron, 94th bomb group, 8th Air Force.

In April 1943 they left New York Harbor for England sailing on the RMS *Mauretania*, one of the largest ships in the world. The former luxury liner converted to a troop ship could hold thousands of bodies, many of whom slept in hammocks on the decks.

Arriving in England in May 1943, Seibold and his crew settled at their permanent base at the village of Bury St. Edmunds. The airfield was built for American bomb groups with a 2,000-yard concrete runway.

During the next year, Seibold's crew flew dozens of missions targeting industrial locales, such as Brunswick and Berlin. On June 6, 1944 the crew provided air support during D-Day -- the largest amphibious invasion the world had ever known -- over German-occupied Caen and Bayeux, France.

Their bombing missions continued unthwarted until the morning of October 5, 1944. As the crew neared the IP (initial point or target) near Kersmecke, Germany, all felt it had been an easy mission with no sign of flak (antiaircraft fire). The bombardier prepared to release the bombs when suddenly the plane received a jolt.

Looking out his window, Seibold was shocked to see flames covering the plane's left engine. The pilot, Robert Messersmith, calmly spoke to the crew over their earphones: "Brace yourselves. We're going into a dive."

Allied soldiers march into Germany in March 1945.
National Archives

From their training the crew knew when a plane was in trouble to lighten its load, thus increasing their chances of traveling closer to Allied territory. Out the jump door went guns, ammunition and other loose items. Seibold tried to drop the turret ball but couldn't find a wrench to loosen the bolt.

When Messersmith and the plane's co-pilot sustained wounds above their flak suits covering their chests, the other eight members struggled to put them into their parachutes and shove them out the door. Hopefully the officers would land safely.

Then it was Seibold's turn to bail out. He took a few moments to scuff his shoes. "The Army Air Corps had issued heated shoes to flight crews that plugged in to our flight suits to keep our feet warm at high altitudes," he said. "I thought if I bailed out in good-looking shoes, German soldiers would kill me for them."

Thankfully, his chute opened and Seibold landed safely, as did all of his crew members. They watched sadly as their plane crashed in a towering ball of flames.

The men's thoughts took another direction when they were apprehended at gun point -- not by German soldiers, but civilians.

The civilians turned the American crew over to German military officials who claimed they had found guns in the plane's cockpit during a search. Seibold knew this was false as the Army Air Corps had done away with that practice.

The men were interrogated separately in English. When Seibold refused to offer more than his name, rank and serial number, he was threatened with a bayonet, then put into a cell where for several days he received little food. "My Red Cross package was taken away by the guards," he said.

Later, while incarcerated at a facility in Berlin, Seibold's life was threatened by the same men he had trained with as American and British bombers targeted the city day and night. "Berlin was the worst place to be a POW," he said.

After several days, Seibold and other Allied POWs boarded a boxcar. So many bodies were crowded in that it was standing room only. Other than a couple of restroom breaks, the train never stopped. For days the prisoners received little food or water.

When the brakes finally squealed, the men, weak with hunger, disembarked and obeyed instructions to line up. At spying unopened Red Cross parcels on the ground, their faces lit with anticipation.

But it was not to be. Under threat of being bayoneted, the guards forbade the starving men from touching the boxes. Instead, they marched toward buildings approximately a mile in the distance.

Giving the packages one last glance before turning away, the men trudged toward their new prison. Looking over his shoulder, Seibold saw German women, old men and children grabbing the parcels before running off. He supposed they were starving too.

STALAG LUFT III

The train carrying the POWs had arrived at Stalag Luft III, a German prison for captured Western Allied Air Force personnel. It was located 100 miles southeast of Berlin in Zagan, Poland.

Each POW was assigned to a compound. Compounds held 1,500 men housed in dozens of barracks. Seibold's room housed six Americans and nine British flight crew members.

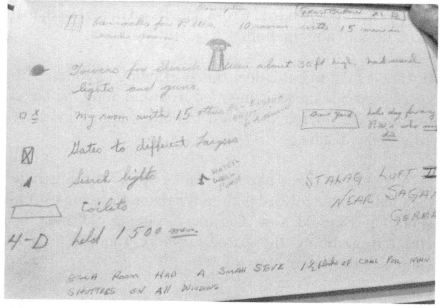

After the war, Seibold created a journal with drawings of his prison camp.

The rooms contained a small stove with one block of coal distributed per prisoner. Shutters covered all of the windows which afforded the men some privacy from the guards in 30-foot-high towers outside.

The searchlights, guns and dogs were meant to intimidate prisoners from escape attempts, although some had been successful in 1943 and 1944.

Curly Seibold was determined to be one of the escapees. For months he watched and waited, though few opportunities presented themselves.

The winter, colder than anyone could remember for that region, passed slowly. The men grew weaker and often sick with diseases.

In December 1944 Seibold wrote to his family on a postcard provided by the guards:

Dear Folks:

Just a line to let you know I am well and ok. We have lots of library books to read so I spend most of my time reading. I sure wish I were home for Xmas. But mebby I will next year. Well, theirs not much to write so will close. Hope this finds you all well. Wilbert.

On February 6, 1945 Seibold and other men in Compound 4-D were told to prepare to leave Stalag Luft III. They would be heading out together on foot for an unknown destination.

The news filled Seibold and the others with dread. Their building, cold though it was, was at least some sanctuary from the frigid outdoor weather.

Rumors for the forced march abounded. Some men deduced it was due to the approaching Russian army. The Germans, now much reduced in manpower from their aggressive invasion of Russia in 1941 when they killed millions, were choosing to run, rather than fight.

Seibold had discovered Dean, another POW, who also wanted to escape. The two met clandestinely to plan. Glancing at the exhausted men who lay on hard-packed snow after walking for weeks, filthy and disheartened, Seibold wondered if he and Dean could sustain the challenges of survival on their own with frigid weather and inadequate clothing, no food or map.

In the end they decided they could not continue to live as they did. It took little effort to slip away unnoticed from the massive group as the guards appeared bored and inattentive.

For several hours Seibold and Dean kept up a steady pace westward toward the Allied front, alert for edible plants and fields of potatoes or cabbages to sustain their energy.

Convinced they were not being pursued, they stopped to rest and sleep, resuming their trek under cover of night. During daylight, the men stayed hidden in ditches and shadows and trees.

One day, upon meeting a group of Polish farm workers, they accepted pieces of clothing for disguises. Through stilted language and gestures, the workers pointed to the railroad in the distance, possibly indicating the Americans should follow the tracks to the Allies.

It sounded like a plan. Outfitted in simple shirts and pants, the men walked along the tracks as though on their way to a work site. But when a German soldier spotted the pair, he demanded at gunpoint that they stop.

Seibold and Dean sank to their knees in despair. Desperately hungry and with nothing to overtake the soldier, they obeyed the order. The thought of returning to another place of captivity depressed them. Could they continue to survive as POWs?

During his time as a PW, Curly Seibold was issued German dog tags. After the war, he kept them as a reminder on a key ring.

The pair didn't know it, but their luck was about to change.

The German guard took them to a village where an interrogator demanded information in English about their service in the Army Air Corps, including names of military officials. When the Americans refused to comply, the official told them he would lock them in a large wire cage.

Something niggled at Seibold about the interrogator. He appeared to be a civilian -- perhaps a Burgomeister (mayor) of the village. As the older man began searching through his pockets, presumably to look for a key, he became increasingly irritated.

Finally giving up the idea that the key was on his person, he sternly instructed the young men to remain in place while he went inside his office to search for the keys.

As soon as he disappeared through the door, Seibold and Dean took off running toward a nearby forest. They had little idea which direction to go but motivation spurred their steps.

The pair walked at night, staying in barns if any could be found but otherwise sleeping outside. The fates seemed to be against them as they spotted yet another German guard who pointed his gun at them, then towards a large building.

The harried men, now nearly overcome with fatigue, staggered to the solid-looking structure. It was, they would discover, a Hungarian prison.

At the beginning of the war Hungary had been part of the Axis powers. Now they were preparing to surrender to the Allies.

The Hungarians offered Seibold and Dean food, haircuts and razors for shaving. There was a reason for their generosity. They needed the Americans' help.

A bombed rail station used by the Nazis in Haguenau, France limits their ability to move materials, a devastation for the German regime. Keith McComb

Based on information they had received, the Hungarians knew a nearby British unit was planning to attack the camp. As the Hungarians within the camp were ready to surrender, there was no need for the attack. Would Seibold write a letter to the British officials, explaining the situation and asking the Allies not to bomb the camp? A Hungarian envoy would deliver it.

Seibold agreed. The letter had the desired result. When British troops arrived at the camp, they locked up the Hungarians and freed Seibold and Dean.

British military officers conveyed to Seibold that had the letter not arrived when it did, they would have demolished the camp.

Seibold and Dean gleefully rode with British troops on a tank to the Allied front line. They happily joined other POWs who had been liberated by Allied troops.

By now, the war was nearly over. Thousands of Germans soldiers had surrendered and Allied troops freed thousands of Allied soldiers from around the world in other prisoner of war camps.

The task of sending home Allied troops commenced. Priority was given to POWs. Seibold arrived at Camp Kilmer in New Jersey in the fall of 1945. At Camp Atterbury in Indiana he was discharged and awarded a number of medals, including an air medal and a Purple Heart.

After the war, Seibold visited the family of a former crew member from Otis, Indiana, who had died during a mission. "Tom and I were close buddies and it hit me hard when he was killed in action," Seibold told the grieving parents.

When the family brought Tom's Purple Heart, issued posthumously, into the room, everyone in the family stood. Seibold was profoundly moved by the gesture of love and respect.

Seibold married and worked at a local factory. In 2015 a piece of his downed aircraft adhered to a plaque was given to him by an appreciative friend. Seibold treasures the gift as well as a photo of his flight crew. He is the only remaining member. He carries German dog tags issued to him during his imprisonment on a keychain.

"My time in the war was interesting, but I would not want to do it again," he said.

Note: The 94th Bomb Group flew 324 missions in 8,884 sorties from May 1943 to April 1945. The crew dropped 18,924 tons of bomb while losing 153 aircraft.

Jerry Wolf – Army Air Corps

Falling from the sky at 20,000 feet was like nothing Jerry Wolf had ever imagined. Clouds surrounded him, making it seem as though time and motion had stopped. Jerry imagined he could hear organ music around him.

Reality set in when a forest with tall trees appeared below. Wolf pulled his parachute's lines, not wanting to get hung up in the branches. He directed his body toward a large bush and farmhouse, hoping to land somewhere flat.

Wolf managed not to break a leg, but he had no time to escape as a man ran out of the house carrying a rifle. The man pointed the gun in Wolf's direction.

"Pistole! Pistole!" he shouted. Wolf shook his head. Flight crews had stopped carrying pistols in chute shoulder holsters when the guns broke too many jaws by flying up during descent.

The fact was, Jerry had no pistol, nor anything else to protect himself.

How quickly everything changed. In a matter of minutes Wolf had gone from a relaxed state of being to one of extreme fear.

He had traded his designation of B-17 gunner with the 390th Bomber Group / 570th Bomb Squadron of the 8th Air Force to a prisoner of war.

Jerry Wolf hoped he could survive.

Jerry Wolf didn't know where Pearl Harbor was located. But upon hearing thousands of American sailors had been killed there by the Japanese on December 7, 1941, he was ready to fight for America.

Born in 1924, Wolf lived with his father, David, mother Sonia and older sister Ruth in Brooklyn, New York. David Wolf owned a heating and plumbing company. Jerry worked for his father after attending classes at Jefferson High School. Jerry hoped someday to attend college to become a chemist.

He was in a pool hall with friends on December 7, 1941, when news of the Japanese attack at Pearl Harbor was announced on the radio. Wolf and his friends didn't know where Pearl Harbor was, but they knew their country would be going to war and they would become soldiers.

For a while life went on. After graduating in May 1942, Wolf enrolled at Brooklyn College. When many of his professors were drafted, Wolf figured it was just a matter of time before the same happened to him.

The idea of becoming a soldier grew on him, especially when college officials informed male students that if they enlisted, they would receive credit for completing the semester.

That sounded good. A few weeks earlier, Marine recruiters had told the male students they should wait to become Marines. Right then that branch's quota was full.

Wolf didn't want to be a Marine. At Thanksgiving 1942 he signed up for the Army Air Corps.

His mother worried Jerry would die in a plane crash. She made him promise to never fly. To appease her Jerry promised he would be an aircraft mechanic. That promise turned out to be difficult to keep.

In January 1943 Wolf traveled by troop train from Camp Upton in New York to Miami, Florida, for basic training. He and other recruits stayed in a beautiful hotel on the beach.

From there it was to Amarillo Army Air Field in Texas where he learned aircraft mechanic training. He also experienced how misinformation could create fear.

One day after their training was completed, six soldiers including Wolf, walked down a street in Amarillo. Upon meeting four young women, they stopped to chat.

Suddenly, one of the girls started to cry. A guy in the group yelled to Wolf, "Hey, Jerry, show her you don't have horns. She thinks Jews have horns."

Wolf had not encountered much anti-Semitic behavior while growing up in New York. Now, far from home in service to his country, he was viewed as a monster.

Putting the ugly incident out of mind, Wolf focused on his gunnery practice in B-17s.

The B-17 was a long-range bomber that could travel 2,000 miles at an altitude of 35,600 feet. With a cruising speed of 180 miles per hour and maximum speed of 287 miles per hour, it carried heavy defensive armament, enabling even badly damaged B-17s to safely return to base.

The B-17 had the reputation of dropping more bombs than any other American aircraft in World War II. Of approximately 1.5 million tons of bombs dropped on Nazi Germany and its occupied territories by U.S. aircraft, over

640,000 tons were dropped from B-17s. It could also be used as a transport, antisubmarine aircraft and search-and-rescue aircraft.

Jerry Wolf's relationship with girlfriend Dottie Ferber prior to the war sustained him through months of being a POW.

Wolf liked gunnery training. Each gunner was assigned an individual color of wet paint on the end of his 50-caliber machine gun bullets. When firing at targets, the colors indicated gunners who required more practice.

Wolf was happy when his shots were dead-on. The gunners also learned to break down the plane's machine guns blindfolded, becoming familiar with every part.

Next, Wolf was sent for advanced training at Boeing Aircraft in Seattle, Washington. Six months later, he was declared a specialist on B-17s and B-29s.

In Salt Lake City, Wolf graduated from gunnery training and received his wings, signifying he was ready to join a flight crew.

But first he had to make a trip.

Wolf had been gone from home for a year. His family had never seen him in uniform. He wrote regularly to his girlfriend, Doris 'Dottie' Ferber and wanted an opportunity to ask her in person to wait for him until the war was over to get married.

It didn't appear that opportunity would occur as crews were not allowed leave time before being sent overseas.

Then came the marvelous news that the order had been changed -- crews who would be flying combat missions were granted a nine-day delay in route!

In January 1944, carrying all of his belongings, Wolf traveled to New York. Seeing his family was great. Having Dottie accept his friendship ring made him feel proud and grown up. Too soon it was back to military business.

After riding a troop train to Ardmore, Oklahoma, Wolf was assigned to a B-17 flight crew. The B-17 carried 10 members: pilot, co-pilot, bombardier/nose gunner, flight engineer/top turret gunner, radio operator, two waist gunners, tail gunner, and ball turret gunner under the plane.

Everyone on a B-17 was a gunner, except the pilot and co-pilot. The crew manned 50-caliber machine guns that turned 360 degrees and could put out a lot of bullets when needed.

Wolf was originally assigned as a waist gunner. When his pilot, A. J. Mathias, discovered Wolf had trained at Boeing, he moved Wolf behind him as flight engineer to give directions.

For a long time Wolf and the other members of his crew wondered what A.J. Mathias' initials stood for. When they found out 'A' stood for "Adolph", they decided to call him 'Sir.'

As a former P-38 fighter, Matthias found guiding the B-17, which the crew nicknamed 'Mountaineer', was like steering a pregnant Mack truck.

The crew practiced with the plane's Norden bombsight, a computer device that enabled a flight crew to drop bombs on a target with unprecedented accuracy from high altitudes. Using variables locked in by the bombardier, the Norden could measure the aircraft's ground speed and direction to determine the point at which the aircraft's bombs should be released to hit the target.

Approximately 45 minutes before the formation's lead plane approached the Initial Point (IP), the crew turned on the Norden. During the bomb run, the plane would be on autopilot and the bombardier would release six 1,000-pound bombs.

Wolf's crew practiced with 100-pound sand bags to achieve a high degree of accuracy.

One tactic to ensure safety for flight crews was to fly in formation at a high altitude. But flying at such a high altitude caused the temperature inside the plane to drop as low as minus 50 degrees.

To avoid frostbite the crew wore heated flight suits that could be plugged in and adjusted with a rheostat. Their hands were protected by two types of gloves – silk and leather. The gloves could be removed for toilet purposes before being quickly replaced.

Jerry Wolf (standing, far left) flew 24 missions with the crew of the 390th Bomb Group before their plane, the Mountaineer, was shot down.

In March 1944, Wolf's crew received its overseas orders – they were headed to Europe. From Kearney, Nebraska, they ferried their B-17 from Maine to Newfoundland, then across the Atlantic Ocean to Scotland. Their final destination was the 390th Bomber Group / 570th Bomb Squadron base at Framingham in Suffolk, England, north of London. The 390th's targets were aircraft factories, bridges and oil refineries.

On mission days crews were awakened at 0200 hours (2:00am) with breakfast at 0300. Take-off was 0700 hours. Most missions lasted between six and 10 hours.

Crews not only fought Germans anti-aircraft fire and planes, but also weather and idiosyncrasies of the planes, which not even the most thorough ground crews could prevent.

During spring 1944, Mountaineer's crew flew 24 bomb missions over Germany. The men recognized each mission was an appointment with death. The evidence was around them daily.

Despite heavy armament and high altitudes, hundreds of B-17s were intercepted by Luftwaffe fighters. On October 14, 1943, an attempt on ball-bearing factories in Schweinfurt, Germany, resulted in appalling losses. Of 291 Fortresses that left their bases that day, 60 were shot down over Germany. Five made it to England, only to crash on approach.

More than 100 bombers needed repairs and twelve were scrapped due to damage. Only 33 bombers landed without damage.

Even more devastating was the loss of flight crews. Of the 2,900 who manned their aircraft, approximately 650 did not return; the day became known as "Black Thursday."

The main problem was antiaircraft fire, or flak. The Germans knew the B-17s altitude and speed. They shot .88 shells with high-tech devices called proximity fuses. A proximity fuse, sensing a target mid-air, caused its shell to explode. That sent pieces of shrapnel into the plane's engines, forcing the plane out of formation.

At some point Wolf was moved to the top turret. From there he could view 360 degrees. Every crew member reported to him if an enemy plane was spotted.

The crew used the clock system. If the tail gunner said, "Airplane, airplane, six o'clock low," that meant he had spotted a plane from behind. He would watch until the plane was identified as friend or foe. If the latter, everyone's guns were trained at it.

To distract German radar Wolf tossed out pieces of silver paper, a simple diversionary tactic called chaff that proved surprisingly effective.

SHOT DOWN

On May 28, 1944, Wolf's crew was not scheduled to fly. At the last minute the pilot volunteered his crew for a mission -- bombing an oil refinery at Magdeburg, Germany.

Due to the last-minute notification, the crew was delayed departure by one hour. Still, Wolf's crew progressed to the target with no problems.

As they reached the initial point, suddenly a German Messerschmitt (ME) 109 jet came out of the sun, the high-technology aircraft moving faster than Wolf's turret mechanism could track.

The Mountaineer and other B-17s in the formation flew undaunted toward their targets, 20-millimeter shells struck Mountaineer's number 1 and 2 engines on the left side.

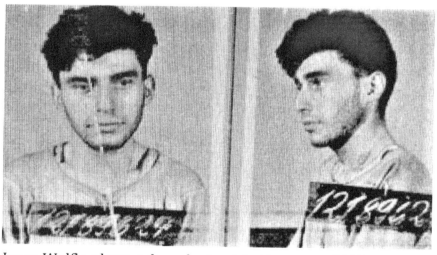

Jerry Wolf's photo taken during his time as a POW reveals more than the need of a haircut and shave – possibly the beginnings of a despondent spirit.

The explosion threw Wolf off of his pedestal in the top turret. As he fell into the body of the plane, he screamed in agony. Something had pierced his leg – probably a piece of shrapnel. The same piece severed his intercom and oxygen lines, preventing his crew from hearing his distress.

Mathias and co-pilot Henry Gerards dropped the plane's bombs to keep them from exploding. They then feathered the propeller. As a last, desperate move, the pair transferred fuel from one engine to another.

At the same time the bombardier sprayed the plane's fire extinguisher to douse the fire that had erupted in the wing where fuel tanks were located. At noticing the crew's navigator had incurred an injury in his leg, the bombardier turned the extinguisher's stream on the limb, hoping the ice-cold contents would freeze the tissue.

The pilots finally gave up. The plane was losing altitude. There was nothing more they could do to save it. The important thing now was to exit safely.

When Gerards noticed Wolf lying on the floor of the plane, he pointed to his own chest. Wolf thought the co-pilot wanted to know if he was injured. Wolf pointed to his bleeding leg. Gerards repeated the gesture and Wolf finally understood. Gerards wanted Wolf to don his Mae West life vest. It was time to bail out.

Wolf and Gerards helped each other snap on their chutes. The bomb bay hatch was built on a curve making it necessary to grab the top of the hatch and kick one's self out to exit. The bombardier and navigator had already jumped. The radio operators and gunners were headed out the plane's back exit.

Taking a deep breath, Wolf kicked the hatch. Screaming to relieve pressure in his eardrums, he plunged his body into the unknown.

Due to a lack of oxygen, Wolf blacked out. When he came to, his body was bouncing. Unsure how long he had been unconscious, he counted to 20, making sure he was away from the plane, before pulling on his chute. As he raised his hands to guide the lines, red drops flew through the air. It was then Wolf realized not just his leg had been injured -- his left arm had been pierced as well.

Although Wolf could have continued with the relaxing, dreamlike state of floating 20,000 feet in the air, the appearance of a ME-109 racing at him erased his somnolence. The pilot completed a perilously close 180-degree turn that left Wolf swinging wildly.

It was an unspoken maneuver German pilots used. By not shooting at Allied crew members, they could not be blamed when the slipstream caused the bodies to swing higher than the chute, thus collapsing it.

Wolf had no time to dwell on ethics as he hit the ground near the farmhouse. After a few moments, he looked up to see an armed man with his gun pointing steadily at Wolf.

CAPTURED

With nothing to defend himself, Wolf marched in front of his captor. In despair he thought of how the news of his downed plane would devastate his mother.

The guard took Wolf to a building for interrogations. The questioning lasted several days. The questions spoken in German made Wolf think of conversations with his grandmother in Yiddish. He pretended not to understand, although he feared his background would come to light soon.

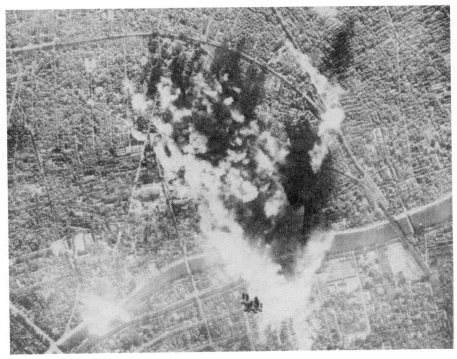

The mission of this B-17 Flying Fortress of the 8th AAF Bomber Command had been to attack a ball-bearing plant and aircraft engine repair depot in Paris, December 1943. National Archives

Each soldier's dog tag was stamped with a religious preference for burial rites. Wolf's dog tag had the letter 'H' for Hebrew. Wolf had chosen not to have it changed,

119

although it had been suggested at the time of issue. He was the only Jewish member of the flight crew.

Wolf also carried a Jewish Bible and family pictures. Although he had been bar mitzvah'd, he had in recent years flaunted his Jewish heritage.

Wolf's chute harness contained four pouches of survival items: money, silk maps, language card and sulfa packet. He used the sulfa to treat his leg and arm injuries. Handling the language card convinced his interrogators of his inability to communicate. By listening furtively, Wolf learned he was at Dulag Luft near Frankfurt.

He joined hundreds of Allied flight crew members herded on to a train, 70 men to a car. For days they rode with no stops to exercise, use a latrine or drink water. Thankfully, air circulated around the cars via ill-fitting beams overhead. The stench of closely confined bodies became palpable. Unaware of the Allies' presence within, American pilots fired on the train, nearly killing some of their own countrymen.

STALAG LUFT IV

On June 6, 1944, the train stopped at Stalag Luft IV in eastern Poland. Wolf quickly thought of it as 'The Place of No.'

There was no hot water or heat in the dirty barracks, no showers, basins, wash tub, toilet paper, brooms, towels and no food.

The prisoners were told to strip, then received a pair of underwear, pants, shirt, overcoat, and two blankets. Wolf wore those clothes constantly for a year.

In one small room 24 men were assigned 12 double bunks with mattresses filled with hay and bugs. The first thing the men traded for was barber shears to shave their heads against lice. A 2-slit (hole) latrine provided their toilet needs.

Roll call took place three times a day, no matter the weather. In winter, a pot belly stove in the barracks gave forth a measly amount of warmth.

Each morning the prisoners received one slice of moldy bread and what was referred to as 'herbal' tea. The rest of their diet consisted of watery soup, potatoes, kohlrabi, rutabaga, or horse meat. They were given second helpings when others turned theirs down, usually due to poor health.

Their diet was supposed to be supplemented with Red Cross packages, but that rarely occurred, due to the guards' stealing the contents.

Each day the prisoners filled aluminum pitchers from outside pumps for drinking. If caught washing their bodies or brushing teeth, they were punished.

At night guard dogs prowled the area to discourage escape attempts. The prisoners had been briefed during flight training to try to escape. That was easy to say but hard to do. Wolf never knew of tunnels being dug or other escape attempts by prisoners in Stalag Luft IV.

With poor sanitation many prisoners, including Wolf, suffered from diarrhea and dysentery. A German doctor treated them with limited supplies. Wolf was impressed with the doctor's skill in treating his injured arm with no scar resulting.

Other maladies -- empty stomachs, cold, fear -- kept the prisoners awake at night, combining to convince them they

American pilots trained in all types of Allied aircraft, including Avengers. They spent hours learning to fly in formation and other maneuvers before heading overseas to fight in combat, September 1942. National Archives.

had been forgotten by families and friends and would probably not survive.

MAIL

Prisoners at Stalag Luft IV were allowed to send two letters and two postcards per month. Incoming mail was unlimited. Desperately missing his family, Wolf wrote to Doris and his family often.

In October 1944 he was overjoyed at receiving the first of what would be 23 letters from home.

In a letter from his sister Wolf learned that a few weeks after he was shot down, his family had received a telegram, listing his status as missing in action. On July 3, 1944, they received another telegram telling of his status as a Prisoner of War.

She added that all 10 families of the crew had been notified of their loved ones' imprisonments. No information was provided of the prison locations. Wolf's family had reported his demise to Doris once they were certain of his status.

With a lack of privacy in the crowded POW camp, Wolf carried all of his personal belongings, including letters, around his waist under a belt. Over time, the letters written in pencil became wet and hard to read.

From January 1945 through June he received no mail. He wondered if the guards had kept his letters.

During the war, the Red Cross helped with notifications of imprisonments. When a soldier was captured in Germany, his dog tag was entered into the international POW system via the German Red Cross.

Kriegies open Red Cross packages under the watchful eyes of two 'goons' – German guards.

The information was sent to the Swiss Red Cross and finally the American Red Cross who relayed it to the American Defense Department.

The Red Cross provided other materials to the prisoners, including books, cigarettes, cans of Spam, bully beef (finely minced corned beef in a small amount of gelatin), D-bar (a high-calorie chocolate bar that would not melt in high temperatures), tuna fish, crackers, vitamins and powdered milk. The milk was considered by many to be highly desired as it was closest to the real thing.

Each package was to provide sufficient nutrition for one person for one week. As the packages were delivered irregularly, the prisoners surmised the German guards kept them. In a show of camaraderie, the men rationed the packages among themselves so the parcels ended up being enough for two people for three weeks.

The Red Cross also provided books for the men to read. In good weather the men organized softball games, playing between barracks for their World Series.

In a strange sort of way, Wolf didn't view his imprisonment as all bad. Inside the camp walls he didn't have to deal with the fear of flying bombing missions. No one shot at him, nor was there flak and noise. He never saw a burning plane or have to count the chutes that emerged from a damaged plane. In between roll calls he could sleep and walk.

The arrival of cribbage and Monopoly was another way to dispel boredom as the men spent hours playing the board games. But the games secretly served another purpose -- one that Wolf and many other prisoners never knew about until after the war.

One particular cribbage board had a built-in radio. The Monopoly game housed secret maps. In the right hands, both helped the Allied war effort, even from inside the camp. Prisoners made an effort to befriend guards operating the prison post office, ensuring the games got through.

JEWISH BIBLE

One morning, the Camp Commander sent for Wolf. This terrified the young man who feared his Jewish background had finally been reported. The prisoners had heard that European Jews were being killed by the thousands. Would that be his fate?

To Wolf's immense relief the Commander didn't want to kill him. In fact, he asked for Wolf's help.

Wolf's ability to understand the German language had been detected. The Commander asked for his help in translating interviews with Allied flight crews. In exchange, the Commander would return Wolf's Jewish prayer book which had been confiscated at his capture, along with personal effects and family photos.

Wolf agreed. One week later his photos and prayer book were returned. The latter was stamped "gepruft", which meant it had been approved by the camp commander. It would never leave his side.

Wolf read the Bible often. He prayed for his family and friends. He loaned the Bible to Catholic POWs who read Hebrew.

The winter of 1944-1945 set records for cold temperatures and several feet of snow. One morning in January Wolf asked to see the guard of his unit. He and other men in the barracks were freezing, even while wearing all of their clothing and blankets. Their barracks stove failed to work due to the lack of a chimney.

With Wolf's background in plumbing, he had thought of a way to use empty powdered milk cans to form a chimney for the stove. The guard agreed to help. Wolf's design idea worked and soon his enclosed area was burning coal and expelling heat to the beleaguered men.

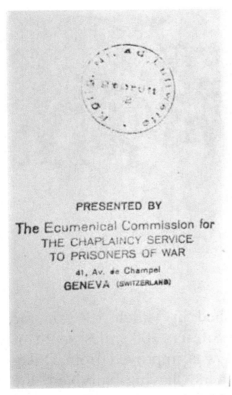

PRESENTED BY
The Ecumenical Commission for
THE CHAPLAINCY SERVICE
TO PRISONERS OF WAR
41, Av. de Champel
GENEVA (SWITZERLAND)

Jerry Wolf read his Jewish Bible often as a POW.

BLACK MARCH

By late winter, the German regime was growing increasingly nervous. They had run out of food, supplies, tanks, and men. Still, their Fuhrer, Adolf Hitler, refused to surrender.

As Russian troops approached from the East, the German high command instructed its camp commanders to move their prisoners.

Upon hearing the news that they should prepare for a move, Jerry Wolf was devastated. He expected a package from home -- salami and clean clothes.

127

The Commander, knowing of Wolf's disappointment, gave him a Greek and Hebrew Bible with the five books of Moses. Wolf appreciated the gesture but still dreaded the journey.

For 68 days Wolf and hundreds of other prisoners marched 60 miles southeast to Stalag Luft III near Nuremberg. Due to the distance and weather, the torturous trip became known as the 'Black March.'

Newly-captured Allied POWs enter Dulag Luft, ca. 1943.

Stalag Luft III was established in March 1942 in the German province of Lower Silesia, 100 miles south of Berlin. Nothing in the camp was improved from Dulag Luft. The exhausted prisoners, having survived the arduous trek, settled in for more hunger-filled days.

In mid-April a guard informed the POWs of the death of Franklin D. Roosevelt. This was the only president most of the young American men had ever known. He had just begun an unprecedented fourth term (the only president who ever would) when on April 12, 1945, he died of a brain hemorrhage.

The new president -- Roosevelt's Vice-President, former Kansas State Senator Harry S. Truman – was unknown to most of America. As Truman assumed control of the country and the war, the POWs wondered, like most other Americans, how much he would do for the war. Wolf hoped the new president would end the war soon and free the POWs.

Amazingly, the German guards allowed Wolf and the other Americans a few moments of silence in respect for the death of their beloved American president.

In early 1945 a rumor circulated that the Russian Army was approaching Stalag Luft III. They had suffered terribly at the hands of the Germans and now were out for revenge.

On April 27, Jerry Wolf turned 21. He had spent the past 10 months of his life as a prisoner of war. He hoped he would not have to spend another year of his life as a POW.

A fantastic event occurred two days later when American tanks came rolling through the camp. They belonged to General George S. Patton's Third Army. It was the best birthday present Wolf had ever received!

Most of the German guards had run away from their posts at the camp. Those that remained were quickly apprehended.

The newly liberated soldiers had to wait a few weeks for the massive evacuation process to be organized. Finally in June 1945, Wolf arrived at Camp Lucky Strike at Le Havre, France.

Every man was deloused and weighed. Wolf was uncertain how much weight he had lost in the camp but knew it was considerable. After a few weeks of medical attention, he was well enough to travel.

Wolf's trip on the USS *Admiral Benson*, took five days.

As the vessel approached New York Harbor, Wolf ran to the ship's rail. When he saw the Statue of Liberty, tears welled in his eyes. He was home!

Tech Sergeant Wolf's official discharge from the Army occurred in October 1945. Everyone in his crew of 10 survived the imprisonment. They stayed in touch for a while after the war but never met for a reunion.

Jerry Wolf and Doris married in 1947 and became parents to three children. He worked as a project manager and took night courses at Brooklyn College to complete a degree in education.

For many years Wolf didn't talk about his WWII experiences. His sister saved his letters and newspaper articles and put them together for a complete history.

"We POWs learned to live with each other," he said. "We had different ideas and religions and political views and sometimes we got angry with each other, but we always cooled off. Most important to us was the will to live. That grew stronger each day in all of us."

Granville ("Grant") Workman – Army

"No one can imagine what it would be like to be interned in a prison camp for three years, to be beaten and tortured, worked to the point of exhaustion daily and to live in filth and disease. I was one of the few who marched into one of those hellholes and marched out, a survivor."

-- statement from the journal of Grant Workman written after he returned home from military service.

Granville 'Grant' Workman was born in Knox, Indiana, in 1925. In September 1941, feeling the need to escape a difficult family life, he quit school in the 10th grade. The 15-year-old falsified his birth certificate to enlist in the United States Army.

His deception remained undetected and after completing basic training at Fort Benjamin Harrison in Indianapolis, Workman was assigned to Co. I in the Infantry.

Soon, his unit had sailed to the Philippines where things were heating up with the Japanese. Despite his desire to leave home, Workman wrote a letter to his family in early

December 1941, just days before the Japanese attacked Pearl Harbor and the Philippines. The now 16-year-old Workman describes his first days in the Pacific, revealing news that his family may not have been happy to read:

Dear Dad

Just writing a line to let you know where I am. I am in the Philippines Island. How are you and the family? We were a month on water when we came across the Pacific ocean.

The first night on the boat I was seasick and threw up all over as did the rest of the crew, then I was allright. We stopped in Honolulu, Hawaii for 1 night and went there to Dole Pineapple Co.

We also stopped at Guam about half between Hawaii & Philippines. When we got to the Philippines, I was excited to see the town of Manila. But after a day or two I got all of it I wanted.

I would give anything to be back home, but I know I'll never be back, you don't have to tell everyone about it, but I am going out to Fort McKinley for boat and pier training and in six months I am going to China to fight the Japanese.

If we are lucky we will probably have to fight the Russians. But that's enough of that.

I have joined the Military police and am on the firing squad of the 31ˢᵗ Infantry. We have been given a 30-cal. rifle M1 and .45 Colt revolver, a bayonet and such war equipment. We went out on the firing range the other day and I made sharpshooter, next to expert.

I am sending home a lot of things from here as soon as I get paid ... I don't suppose I could get out of the army but if I could I would!

I go to church every Sunday. And nearly everyone in the army smokes and gets drunk about every night but I haven't smoked or even smelled of any beer or liquor or such yet and I'm not going to.

Good luck to you and the rest of the family say hello to them all for me. Hoping you will write as soon as you receive this letter, it only costs 50 by airmail. Well so long. Will send pictures and Christmas presents soon.

Your loving Son

Granville Workman

Workman never had the opportunity to send Christmas presents and pictures to his family. This would be his last letter home for more than three years. Within days Japanese military forces would attack the Philippines, changing his life forever.

(Journal begins)

December 9, 1941

When the first wave of Japanese bombers hit Nichols Field south of Manila in the Philippines, I thought the world was coming to an end. Eight more waves of enemy planes shone searchlights around us, looking and sounding horrifying.

The Japanese were brilliant strategists and fearless fighters. Looking down my M1 rifle sight as I surveyed the area, I recalled doing the same with my grandad's shotgun while shooting rabbits in Indiana. The difference was those rabbits had not returned fire.

I had grown up in a rural area of northern Indiana near Plymouth. I joined the United States Army a few months before my 16th birthday in September 1941, lying about my age on my enlistment.

The world had already heard about the sneak attack by the Japanese on Pearl Harbor on December 7, 1941. By the time the attack was over the following day, most of our P-40's at Nichols Field and B-17's on the ground at Clark Field at Luzon Island had been destroyed. Only a few pursuit planes remained.

The next day 60,000 Japanese troops under the command of Generals Homma Masaharu and Tomoyuki Yamashita landed at Lingayen Gulf. This was on the northwestern side of Luzon, the largest island in the Philippines and location of the country's capital city of Manila. Masaharu was commander of the Japanese invasion forces in the Philippines.

Manila was the site of the main American military base in the Pacific. Clark Field was the primary airbase for fighter aircraft expected to provide defensive cover. With 30,000 Allied Army, Army Air Corps, Navy and Marines on Corregidor we had a good number of trained forces. Most of them consisted of engineers, which were non-combat units, but some had been issued rifles and attached to our outfit.

Marine machine gunners push back Japanese soldiers in a jungle at Cape Gloucester, January 1944. National Archives

Among our troops were two crack Filipino Infantry units – the 45th and 54th. The Filipinos loved the Americans. They called us their 'White Brothers'. We, in turn, called the Filipinos our 'Brown Brothers'. They were terms of affection, rather than racist remarks. We each took pride in the terms.

At one point the Japanese may have hoped to convert the Filipinos to their cause of a united Asia against white colonists. It never happened. The Japanese killed thousands of Filipinos who tried to help the Allies as guerilla military fighters. In addition, many Filipinos died in civilian concentration camps as victims of bayonet practice and other atrocities.

By December 26, Japanese troops were entering Manila. American General Douglas MacArthur, commander of American forces in Manila, declared it an Open City.

Note: A city is declared "open" when while under attack its defensive efforts are abandoned, usually to avoid destruction. Occupying forces are expected to take over peacefully. However, the Imperial Japanese Army ignored the protocol and bombed Manila.

January 1942

Rumors flew about reinforcements arriving to help us. That turned out to be optimistic.

Mid-morning the enemy got a fix on our 155th artillery position. In the distance we heard the salvo of four guns. When shells started landing on top of our outfit about 50 yards in front, it was havoc. Soldiers screamed as they were hit, bushes and clay flying over. For six hours we fired until our original position on the hill was wiped out.

Then someone hollered, "Get off this hill!" We dashed for a ravine.

The USS Arizona burns after the Japanese attack on Pearl Harbor, December 7, 1941. National Archives

Good leadership was paramount. At the onset of the war the commander captain of Co I went AWOL (absent without leave). Our first lieutenant took his place, but although a tough sergeant before the war, he fell to pieces under fire. At the approach of Japanese planes he dove for cover.

In contrast, we had in our company a man named Roy Campbell. During the first attack, he stood and fired from the hip, cutting the enemy down in rows. Boy, did we need more men like him.

We tried to dig foxholes for cover, but the ground was too soft and many boys had lost their trench tools (shovels) when on the move. The guys used whatever they could find to dig – bayonets, mess kit lids, spoons.

In late afternoon the shelling abruptly stopped. With relief we re-organized, getting our gear together and holding our position until dark. Suddenly, a horde of enemy soldiers raced out of the jungle yelling "Bonsai!"

Our platoon sergeant hollered for us to retreat to a mountain visible in the evening light. "It's every man for himself," he warned. "If you make it, we'll assemble there."

Two soldiers and I ran through the jungle, each carrying rifles and ammo. It's amazing what strength and effort a soldier can muster when comrades are around. It would have been terribly lonesome and scary to be out there alone.

We made it to the mountain. Next morning, we came on the rest of the 31st along Balanga, the capital of the province of Bataan near the ocean. For the next couple of weeks, we fought skirmishes against what we were told was 60,000 troops under the command of Masaharu and Yamashita. It was evident American forces had never faced such a fanatically determined fighting machine.

A United States Army Forces in the Far East radio station in Corregidor was our only connection with the outside world. Its news built morale with promises of reinforcements which we needed with Japanese bombers flying over in waves daily. When the Zeros strafed, coming in thick and low, we could see pilots grinning at us.

Note: The Zero, manufactured by Mitsubishi, was the first carrier-based fighter capable of besting its land-based opponents. In 1940, the year production began, the 2,600th anniversary of the ascension to the throne of Japan's legendary first emperor occurred, hence the "Zero" classification.

An American tank smashes through a jungle on a South Pacific island while infantrymen follow, March 1944. National Archives.

Once a group came close to our lines, not dropping bombs, but small packages. Inside were firecrackers the enemy used as machine-gun nest decoys. In others were packets of some sort of dope.

We were in foxholes an hour later when the Japanese attacked. At dark, I heard a guy yelling for help. Tiny, a big machine-gunner with a pockmarked face, was trying to feed ammo into an air-cooled machine gun. His assistant who would have fed the bullets had been killed.

I ran over. As Tiny sprayed lead, I fed that gun. When it got hot and jammed, we used a water-cooled machine gun until it jammed and we resorted to rifles.

Later, Tiny found a BAR (Browning automatic rifle) which he used to shoot at the enemy. We were lucky as we were never hit.

That night orders came down to retreat and we set up a new line in the rear. I bumped into Major Bill O'Donovan. He was called 'Wild Bill' because he always carried three Colt .45's — one on each side of his body and in the rear – and a heavy BAR on each shoulder. This one-man army led his troops, chanting 'Charge, men!" You never saw Wild Bill in the rear when there was action.

Note: This is a different "Wild Bill" Donovan than the founder of the Office of Strategic Services (OSS) which later became the CIA.

Wild Bill wanted me as his company runner carrying messages from him to headquarters (HQ). It seemed risky, but what could I say?

We found a grove of mango trees. Wild Bill told me to rest and he would wake me when needed.

The next morning I awoke to find myself alone. With my M1 I started through the jungle. Everything was deathly quiet. Afraid of encountering the enemy, I ran until exhausted.

Pitch black jungle growth surrounded me. At the sound of footsteps, I stepped out and stuck a rifle in someone's stomach, hollering, "Halt!"

With relief I heard a voice cry, "Don't shoot." My prisoner was a captain from the 45th Filipino regiment. Lowering my gun, I asked if he knew of the whereabouts of Wild Bill.

He didn't, but added there was nothing ahead but enemy troops. We turned and ran until dawn. I wondered if the morning star leading us was the same that shone over our family farm back in Indiana.

At a clearing with five tanks on a hill we bellycrawled close to see if they were ours or the enemy's. Relieved to spot American military stars painted on the sides, we identified ourselves to the troops. They told me my outfit was camped in a small barrio called Pilar. I located the outfit at Pilar in time for breakfast.

Like most soldiers, we hated to miss meals. Usually the chow truck arrived at 11:00 pm with bowls of stew. We supplemented our diets with bananas, pineapple, mangos and monkeys if we could catch them.

After breakfast, we moved inland to establish a new resistance line and plug a hole where the Japanese had broken through. Throughout the day, bombers pounded and Zeros strafed. With all of the lead and steel they threw at us, it seemed Bataan would break off and sink into the ocean.

At daybreak a Co. I man named Smith and I were called on to be scouts, surveilling until the enemy was contacted. It was a risky assignment. One of us was sure to be hit by an enemy bullet.

Moving to a vantage point 50 yards ahead of Smith, I saw nothing unusual and motioned for him to approach. Together, we moved down a gully along the dried-up creek bed. Smith started up the other side.

He had nearly reached the top when a machine gun burst in front of him. Our outfit rushed in and we stayed busy for hours before the enemy retreated. This was the first time we had seen them back off.

I ran to Smith. The coffee cup-sized hole in his helmet assured me he never knew what hit him.

After a spell to rest, I joined six men as part of a patrol to find the Japanese lines. We found a foxhole, which had been a camouflaged machine gun nest but no troops.

As we started back to report our findings, a guy who I think was named Stobaugh and I entered a clearing of mango trees. Suddenly, rifle fire raged, bullets spattering around us.

American troops land at the Solomon Islands for an invasion, June 1943. National Archives

We hit the ground. When American troops attacked the mango grove, Stobaugh and I were caught in No Man's Land between our forces and the enemy.

We could not escape. The only thing to do was play dead until dark or the Japanese pulled back. At one point there was a burning in my right thigh. I guessed a bullet must have creased me.

When it seemed safe to crawl into the gully, I saw Stobaugh had been hit in the groin, a mean-looking chunk of meat missing from his inner thigh.

Another soldier and I used an army shelter half (tent) to rig up a stretcher to carry Stobaugh back to the camp field hospital. Medics took him and other wounded on stretchers to a big tent hospital five miles to the rear. By the time the wound to my leg was tended and I had returned to my outfit, supper was over. That was disappointing.

For many days our outfit zigzagged single-file through the jungle. We stayed 20 yards apart, hoping to prevent the enemy from hitting us with small bombs and strafing. We found what had been an American motor pool attacked by Japanese-built Betty bombers. Wounded soldiers lay scattered in the area hollering for help. Sadly, no first-aid was available, but we did as best we could.

Note: The Japanese attack bomber referred to as 'Betty' by the Allies contained a rotund, cigar-shaped fuselage. The Japanese built more of them than any other bomber during World War II.

(journal resumes)

The 45th Filipino outfit was also hit hard. Desperate to provide replacements, our American non-coms (non-commissioned officers) were told they would be promoted to Second Lieutenant if they volunteered for re-assignment to the 45th. No one agreed. Even among the PFC's (Private First Class) there were no takers.

Our company set up another defense line before the enemy could drive us into the ocean. Rumors of reinforcements continued, but no date was given for their arrival.

Some guys could not handle the pressure of combat. When one guy shot himself in the foot, he claimed he was cleaning his rifle when it accidentally discharged. We knew it was no accident as he had said days earlier he would never again go into battle. There were other cases like that.

Food became scarcer. We were hungry enough to eat pineapples with stickers which made our mouths bleed.

Infantrymen use flame throwers on the Marshall Islands, February 1944. National Archives

One morning we heard a rustling in a bamboo clump. Thinking it was the enemy, a group of us surrounded the bush, rifles ready. When a python slithered out, we breathed in relief. That evening we enjoyed python steaks.

One afternoon we found a stream while climbing a mountain. We drank and filled our canteens. As we turned a bend, we spotted two dead Japanese soldiers lying dead upstream. No one emptied their canteens.

Cases of malaria, hunger and low morale took their toll. Our forces carried a radio which played the captured radio station of Manila. Their theme song which we heard often didn't help: "I'm Waiting for Ships That Never Come In."

Another voice on the radio -- Tokyo Rose -- tried to convince us to give up. This propagandist repeated reports of American losses and assured her American listeners, should they surrender, they would be treated according to guidelines established at the Geneva Convention. All we needed was to walk toward the Japanese lines, gun barrels pointing to the ground and holding white hankies.

I admit, at times the idea of surrender sounded good. Why were we fighting and dying for people we didn't know? If given a choice, at that point I would have given the Philippines to Japan and returned home.

As it turned out, Tokyo Rose and her program didn't get as many men killed as 'Dugout Doug', the name we gave to Lieutenant General Douglas MacArthur. He commanded the United States Army Forces in the Far East from his headquarters in Manila.

American bombers flew over us daily, dropping pamphlets signed by him, stating "reinforcements had arrived with hundreds of planes and tanks and thousands of men."

The next morning the announcement seemed to be true as we heard planes approaching. Guys jumped out of foxholes, peering through the fog to see if they were ours.

Unfortunately, when the fog cleared, we didn't see stars under the wings identifying the planes as American. The red balls on the planes belonged to Japan's Rising Sun.

Bombs and bullets from the Zeros' continual passes rained on us like hail. We ran for foxholes, but lots of guys didn't make it.

One Zero pilot approached my foxhole, bomb hanging under his plane. Praying with all of my heart that he would miss his target, I hit the ground as the pilot released his bombs.

Dirt chunks spattered around me and explosions hurt my eardrums. I had had little experience with prayer, but it's surprising how hard one can pray when confronted with death. After he flew off, I spied a new crater behind me. I believe my prayers turned those bombs in another direction.

**

March 1942

We were at Cabcaben inland at Manila Bay when informed General MacArthur had obeyed an order to evacuate to Australia with his family. At that point we seemed to be fighting a losing battle.

General Jonathan Wainwright was the new Commander of the Armies of the Philippines. Wainwright appointed General Edward King to command the forces of Bataan.

Japanese bombers pounded our positions from morning to night. Masaharu appealed to Wainwright to surrender, but Wainwright ignored the order.

Finally, on April 9, 1942, it was over. After months of resistance, faced with no reinforcements and lack of food and ammunition, General King offered to negotiate the surrender of the Bataan forces. A month later, battling the same obstacles, Wainwright also conceded defeat.

Word arrived to lay down arms and surrender. It was tough seeing the American flag go down and the Japanese flag go up.

Mixed emotions ranged among the Americans. Some believed Uncle Sam would not let us remain prisoners for long. We were his fighting forces in the Far East. Our officers, perhaps sensing release would not be soon, threw away their shirts with bars of rank as we had heard Allied officers would be executed.

I had thought living as a prisoner could not be worse than what we had gone through with a serious lack of food and always on the run and lack of supplies.

I was never more wrong.

BATAAN DEATH MARCH

Allied prisoners endure hands tied behind their backs along the 65-mile stretch from Bataan to Cabanatuan prison camp, May 1942. National Archives.

It took two days to round up 75,000 prisoners, including 60,000 Filipinos and 9,000 Americans.

According to the Japanese, we were not prisoners of war (POWs). At the Geneva Convention Japan had refused established terms of how to treat prisoners of war. Since we had surrendered, they viewed us as cowards and unworthy of being treated as POWs. We were slaves of the emperor and alive only due to his kindness.

We assembled in lines, four abreast, stretching for miles. When incoming American shellfire from Corregidor rained on the area, we stood for hours as living barriers.

Our destination was a place called Camp O'Donnell, an old Filipino army camp, 90 miles away.

Our captors stripped us of everything except clothes and water in our canteens. Some guys had no canteens.

Through the hot, humid days we marched. The trail was dusty. We were offered no food, water or place to rest. If a sick or weak man fell, he was shot or stabbed by a Japanese guard with a bayonet or hit with the butt of a gun. Some prisoners sat in the middle of the march, hoping other prisoners would help them.

As we were herded through the streets of Lubao, Filipino civilians threw food at us. Before we could reach it, screaming guards ground it under their feet.

The grueling march lasted five days. Ten thousand men perished along the way, including more than 1,000 American troops. Four American officers were beheaded, their dripping heads hanging on guards' bayonets and paraded amongst us.

We Americans had never encountered this kind of vicious treatment of prisoners. During combat, that sort of thing was expected but not after a surrender.

ESCAPE TO CORREGIDOR

A few of us planned to escape. As we marched near a small dry dock at Manila Bay, we spotted a banco (small canoe vessel with outriggers and bamboo poles). It was tied, awaiting repairs.

That night, seven of us got away from our captors and raced to the banco. We were terrified the Japanese would spot us under the moonlight. I was waist high in the water before remembering I couldn't swim. A piece of driftwood helped my escape.

Upon reaching the banco, we paddled toward what we thought were the lights of Manila. This seemed a good idea as the tide was going out.

A few hours later, a large boat with searchlight approached us. We feared it was the enemy until through a megaphone we heard a voice. It was an American gunboat patrolling the waters between Bataan and Corregidor.

The crew took us aboard, clothed and fed us -- the first decent meal we had eaten in months. I knew then I should have joined the Navy instead of the Army.

Americans surrender at Corregidor, May 1942. National Archives.

We were issued weapons and I was assigned to the 4th Marines to defend Corregidor near the entrance of Manila.

I reached my new trench buddies --- three Marines -- the next morning. They had dug into the side of a mountain with sand bags to protect both the entrance and exit in case of a hit.

From our position we could see the entrance to Malinta Tunnel. Below us were cold storage lockers and a pier where small crafts docked. During the next month, we were hit with high-flying bombers and artillery using 105-millimeter shells from Bataan and the Cavite side on the southern shores of Manila Bay.

All we could do was bomb and shell using our big 240-millimeter howitzers set up to traverse a 90-degree point toward the sea. Originally Corregidor was to defend Manila Bay from a seaside attack. Our military had not figured on land and air attacks.

I was at the entrance of our tunnel when a piece of hot shrapnel caught me in the left knee. I pulled it out and limped to the Malinta Tunnel hospital for first aid.

Near midnight on May 5, 1942, the enemy landed at Monkey Point on the other end of Corregidor. They took control of the rear entrance to Malinta Tunnel, blocking the bay with warships.

The base fell to the Japanese on May 6, 1942. From my hiding place I watched for the second time as the American flag was replaced by a Japanese one. It felt like losing your mother or father when your country's flag goes down. You don't have much hope.

It was time to leave. The three Marines and I located a 30-foot boat at the dock. We planned a run for Mindanao, an island 500 miles south of Luzon where American forces were located.

After loading the boat with supplies, gas, food, and water, we waited for a dark night to make our escape.

It never happened.

On May 7, while sneaking down a ravine, a Japanese soldier jumped out, thrusting his rifle with fixed bayonet into my side. My short time of freedom was over.

American prisoners carry ill comrades in make-shift litters on the grueling march from Bataan in May 1942. Abuse from Japanese captors, lack of food and water cause thousands of deaths. Photo captured from the Japanese. National Archives.

BILIBID PRISON

The guard and I marched five miles to Bilibid Prison in Manila, a former civilian prison converted to POW camp.

It seemed as though I had arrived in Hell as I was put in a crowded room with no toilets, running water, beds or bunks. The only food was small amounts of rice.

During the next 30 days, we prisoners battled various ills. Malaria was especially virulent. Chills racked our bodies in the 100-plus degree heat before fever took over.

When my temperature reached 106 degrees, I was given quinine. By the time they loaded us on a boat for Manila, I could walk.

PRISON AT CABANATUAN

June 1942

After a short ride, approximately 8,000 of us were marched to a train headed to the village of Cabanatuan, a distance of approximately 100 miles. The crowded conditions in the boxcars meant we stood during the long journey.

At our arrival, we walked seven miles to the 60-acre prison camp where we were greeted by 20-foot barbed wire fences and guard towers.

Our captors assigned us to 10-man groups. To keep us from trying to escape, we were told if one member failed to show up for roll call, conducted twice daily, the other nine would be executed.

We were all inspected for gold in our teeth. If any was found, guards knocked the teeth from our mouths to melt down the metal.

Prisoners were assigned to two groups -- those healthy enough to work and those who were not. The latter went to the hospital, such as it was with a serious lack of staff and supplies. I went to the work section.

Work detail included gardening a 20-acre area referred to as the 'farm'. We worked from early morning until late evening raising vegetables like radishes and sweet potatoes. It was brutally hot. To make the time pass we sang as we worked:

When the early sunbeams break,

You will wonder when you wake

In what muddy neighborhood

There is work and pleasant food

Planting rice is no fun

Work from morning to the setting of the sun

Cannot stand, cannot sit

Cannot rest a little bit.

Oh, my back is about to break

And my bones with the damp still ache

And my feet are wet and set

With long soaking in the wet.

The guards tried to motivate us to work by saying they would share the vegetables with us. Instead, at harvest they took the edible parts while we got the hard, woody tops. We ate them with our daily allotment of rice.

Sometimes we received soup with sweet potato stems. On rare occasions fish heads were thrown in the soup, eyes floating to the top. We caught worms and grasshoppers to fill our empty bellies. We looked like scarecrows with ribs sticking out.

Our barracks were made of bamboo with nipa (grassy) roofs. They sat on three-foot stilts with open upper and lower bays. No doors or windows protected us from thousands of flies and mosquitoes. We had no mats to sleep on and developed sores on our hips due to rubbing on hard bamboo slats.

Mail sent to Workman from his family is returned after the invasion in the Philippines, leaving them to worry about his safety. Months pass before they hear of his whereabouts.

To the rear of the barracks was the latrine, an eight-hole box on top of the ground. Sick prisoners who could not make it soiled themselves in the loin cloth tied around the waist. It was their only piece of clothing.

Our main source of water was a spigot near the barracks from which we had to be granted permission to drink.

We learned Japanese words to communicate with the guards. If unable to say our prisoner number in the Japanese language during roll call, we were beaten with canes. Several guards had attended school in United States and spoke English. They never failed to find opportunities to tell us daily how low the Americans were and how great they were.

The word for toilet was 'benjo.' While working, sometimes a guard would agree to take us to the latrine and sometimes he wouldn't. Then we had no choice but to mess ourselves.

One day while working in the field I yelled 'benjo.' The guard accommodated. Upon completing my task, I reached for leaves to wipe, not noticing which were picked. Soon, I was hopping around in discomfort. The leaves had been a pepper bush. My guard thought my actions meant a snake had got me.

Prisoners assigned nicknames to the Japanese guards. The most evil one was 'Speedo.' That was what he always hollered at us, so we guessed it was the only word he knew for 'hurry.'

Another bad guard was 'Donald Duck.' He and other guards abused us in various ways. The most common was to hit a prisoner with clubs and rifles. Another was to tie a man's feet together, hang him upside down and pour water in his nose.

I once witnessed a prisoner tied to a rope with the other end tied to a horse. A Japanese officer rode the horse at a gallop, dragging the poor prisoner in the dirt. The guard then tied the man to a cross, leaving him for days until he died.

If an American officer in charge of his barracks tried to defend his men from undue punishment, he could be flogged to death.

Two miserable months passed. Temperatures ranged in the 90's and higher, causing blow flies to swarm around us. Prisoners grew weak with bouts of malaria, dysentery, pellagra, dry beriberi, scurvy, dengue fever, diphtheria, yellow jaundice, wet beriberi and other ailments.

One type of dysentery -- 'amoebic' – was due to a bug infection in the intestines, causing stomach cramps and loose stools.

Wet beriberi was caused from a vitamin B deficiency. It was one of the most dreaded diseases as it caused a patient's feet to swell. Other parts of the body including the heart enlarged so the patient often smothered. Many prisoners in our camp died of wet beriberi.

Due to the vast number of Americans killed overseas, cemeteries were established to pay homage to their memory, ca. 1945. National Archives

When I contracted this dreaded disease, they moved me to the hospital. The hospital had 30 barracks. So many prisoners were brought from the work side that the guards had to place them under the building due to a lack of space.

As if conditions were not already tough, a patient's rations were cut in half. With a poor diet and living conditions, extreme heat and dearth of medical care, most prisoners gave up, hoping death would arrive soon.

Slowly, I recovered from the wet beriberi. But the shrapnel wound on my knee from before my capture never healed. The joint often swelled to twice its normal size and maggots filled the wound.

At first, I detested those big green blow flies laying their eggs. Then I realized they were doing me a favor. By eating the dead and rotten flesh around my wound they kept the infection to a minimum. Nature is a wonderful thing.

Despite our weakened conditions, some of us prisoners yearned to escape. It was a life-threatening risk. One prisoner who was caught sneaking under the fence endured a beating before being forced to dig his own grave and shot to death. The guards laughed at his execution as though they had been at a party. The war was over for that guy. Maybe he was the lucky one.

By August 1942, whatever hope we had of Uncle Sam sending help to Cabanatuan had faded. We heard rumors of prisoner exchanges but it seemed unlikely. The Japanese told us repeatedly that Americans were aggressors and criminals and we were all going to die. If we could have received letters from home, it would have helped our morale.

Torture, disease, forced labor, and lack of medicine took its toll. That fall guards retrieved approximately 150 prisoners each morning who had perished during the night.

Survivors were forced at gun point to dig holes for mass graves.

Sometimes the guards picked up a prisoner who was nearly dead and threw him in the hole for burial. If he tried to crawl out, guards killed him with hard strikes of their rifle butts.

In October I again became ill, this time with malaria. When my fever ran high, accompanied by delirium, I was taken back to the hospital where a beating awaited me. For weeks I lay shivering in the hot sun or burning up with fever. When my hair fell out, it didn't matter. I didn't care to survive.

In November I was dismissed from the hospital and put back to work. Days continued hot and long with no news of rescue or hope of a prisoner exchange. Prisoners who could walk lined up for portions of rice, sometimes standing more than an hour. It reminded me of animals on the farm lining up to be fed. It is hard to describe the disease, pain and suffering we felt.

One morning the guards discovered one of my group of 10 was missing. They gave the rest of us 24 hours to find him or we would be executed. We found him the next morning dead in the swamp at the lower end of the compound. He had probably attempted an escape but died due to ill health.

December 1942

Despite our weakened conditions, some guys never gave up trying to escape.

In between the work and hospital sides were four stacks of hay. They were probably for the horses of Japanese officers. Those men liked to gloat over us from their victorious positions.

Gun crews of a Navy cruiser cover the American landing in the Philippines, December 1944. National Archives.

One night four Americans crawled inside the haystacks to hide. One was the guy named Stobaugh whom I had carried out of danger in Bataan. They waited three days until the guards believed they had escaped. I never heard what happened to them. Hopefully, they made it to freedom.

In the days leading up to Christmas our group of 10 received a food parcel from the American Red Cross. The box contained Spam, candy, raisins, and cigarettes. We split it among us. It was greatly appreciated and served to remind us about good things we used to have.

In 1943, the hospital established three wards: 'o', 'oo', and 'St. Peter's.'

The 'o' ward was for prisoners thought to be contagious. The 'oo' ward contained those with little hope of survival.

'St. Peters' became the diphtheria ward. Few prisoners left except feet first.

Japanese guards wouldn't go near those filthy wards. They left food at the fence, forcing ill patients to crawl for it. Prisoners too weak to reach the outside latrine lay in their excrement. Mice and rats ran rampant. They could have been a source of food if we had had the strength to catch them.

I contracted diphtheria and was admitted to the camp hospital until February 1943. I recovered, but aftereffects set in which were almost worse than the disease. My inability to swallow kept me from eating my little portions of rice and sweet potato vine soups. My weight plummeted to 87 pounds.

I had double vision. My legs and head swelled. Paralysis set in, allowing only my head, feet and hands to move.

I would have perished throughout this period of illness if not for a prisoner named Harrington. This American POW suffered from dry beriberi. His feet hurt so badly he could barely walk. Yet, Harrington managed to go to the hospital each day to feed me. When I prayed to die, he offered encouraging words.

One night during my hospitalization, an American captain came around to check for dead prisoners. He told his orderly to throw me under the barracks for burial detail in the morning. Harrington told him I was not dead. The captain replied, "He will be soon."

When the orderly did as directed, Harrington dragged me, inch by inch, back inside the barracks. He could hardly get around, but he refused to leave me. It must have taken hours.

Somehow I survived. Unfortunately, I have no idea what became of Harrington.

(End of journal)

**

In August 1943 Grant Workman's imprisonment took on an even more deadly turn when he and other POWs were moved to Camp 5-B in Niigata, Japan to perform slave labor in coal yards. Health conditions at Niigata were only slightly better than in the Philippines and treatment from the Japanese guards was just as severe as at the previous camp.

In a newspaper article written in the 1990s, Workman was quoted as saying he and the other prisoners of war were forced to leave the camp at daybreak to walk five miles to work, returning after dark.

'Bulldog' was the nickname the Allied POWs assigned to this Japanese guards, many of whom abused the prisoners daily.

After facing unbearable heat in the Philippines, they trekked through several feet of snow in Japan. Their only issued clothing were grass boots and grass capes.

The POWs worked every day of week, receiving one day off per month. Rations consisted of 'lugaw' -- a rice and barley soup. On occasion prisoners ate grasshoppers.

Of the 500 prisoners at Niigata, Workman estimated that 125 died during the two years he was there.

By June 1945 little hope remained in the minds and spirits of the POWs of ever returning home.

Then, in July, B-29 bombers flew over the camp. In August strafing began and Workman and the others knew they came from aircraft carriers which could not be far away.

More B-29s dumped food and supplies into the camp. A few days later the POWs were liberated and taken to Manila to receive medical aid.

After 41 months as a prisoner of war, Grant Workman, who was still too young to vote or drink alcohol, was free. He had survived!

The dearest wish of this 19-year-old was to return home. But things didn't go as he had hoped.

In October 1945, he was hospitalized. His emaciated body had trouble adjusting to medical treatment. At the time of his enlistment he had weighed 148 pounds. His weight as recorded in the hospital at his liberation was 98 pounds.

Still, Workman displayed a positive attitude in this letter written to his family during his recuperation, possibly with the help of a nurse, in a San Francisco hospital:

Dear Dad, mom & all,

I am back in the hospital. I could not get an extension on my pass. So I'll be home in about a week I hope. Say hello to grandad for me. And if you get any letters for me please put them inside another envelope & send them to me at once. Goodbye for now.

Grant

**

On December 19, 1945, Corporal Granville E. Workman was honorably discharged at Camp Atterbury, Indiana.

After the war, he found a job at McCord's Radiator Shop in Plymouth, Indiana. He married in 1947 and he and his wife, Mary Alice, became parents to two children. The family moved to Wells County in 1964 where he retired. Each day Workman flew the American flag at his home.

Grant Workman died in 1998. Several other relatives would serve in the military.

LETTERS

While he was overseas, Granville's family wrote letters to him, many of which he never received until after the war. This excerpt was posted after the attack on Pearl Harbor and in the Philippines:

Plymouth Indiana.

December 9, 1941

Dear Granville:

Received your letter and was more than glad to hear from you. We wrote you a letter yesterday and forgot to send you any money so we are sending you another one. Granville your Grandpa said you needed any money just write and say how much.

I was so glad to know you don't do the things the other boys do. This is no time to do those things. Granville if you ever prayed in your life pray now. Our God is able to safe to the uttermost.

We are praying for you like we never prayed before. The same God that delivered Daniel out of the lion's den is going to deliver you. Granville I am going to get you a small bible and send it to you later on.

Artillery men lay down a murderous barrage on troublesome Japanese positions in Philippines, April 1945. National Archives.

170

Please write just as soon as you get this letter. We will be waiting to hear from you. If you have a later picture of yourself please send us one. If you need anything don't be one bit afraid to say so.

Would you like a cake or something like that. Your Grandpa gave us this dollar to put in this letter and said if you wanted more say so.

Don't forget to pray. It is going to take prayer and help of God. The church is praying for you. Please write as soon as you get this as I am worried over you. Please don't delay in writing.

Good bye Son

Your loving grandfather

**

Upon learning about Pearl Harbor, Grant's family implored the American government to find him and send him home since he was underage. For several months they worked with an attorney named Floyd O. Jellison from South Bend.

Months passed with no word of his whereabouts or wellbeing. Then the family received this sad note:

War Department

The Adjutant General's Office

Washington

June 19, 1942.

Dear Mr. Workman:

Reference is made to your letter of June 9, 1942, requesting information relative to your son, Private Granville E. Workman, 15,081,808.

I regret to inform you that this soldier is carried on the records of the War Department as missing in action in the Philippines Island since May 7, 1942. He will retain that status until information to the contrary is received.

The words "service suspended" marked on the face of the card which was returned to you by the Post Office Department, means that mail service to the Philippines Island has been suspended indefinitely. This, no doubt, accounts for the fact that you have received no word from your son.

The grief and anxiety which this distressing news will bring is deeply regretted.

Very truly yours,

J. A. Ulio, Major General, The Adjutant General.

**

Finally, after nine months of worry, the family received the dreaded confirmation:

War Department

Army Service Forces
  Office of the Provost Marshal General
  Washington

16 September 1943

Mr. & Mrs. Oscar Workman,
R.R. 3
Plymouth, Indiana

Dear Mr. and Mrs. Workman:

The Provost Marshal General directs me to reply to your letter of August 22, 1943, in regard to your son, Private Granville E. Workman, which has been referred to this office by The Adjutant General.

No information has been received other than the cable from the International Red Cross, Geneva, Switzerland, reporting your son interned in the Philippines Island. It is suggested that you address him as follows:

Private Granville E. Workman,
American Prisoner of War
Interned in the Philippines Islands,
c/o Japanese Red Cross, Tokyo, Japan.
Via: NY, NY.

Due to the uncertainties of war, censorship by the enemy, and transportation difficulties, the delivery of mail from American prisoners of war held by the enemy, cannot be assured.

It is regretted that you were unable to send a package to your son on the S.S. Gripsholm. Under special arrangements, however, the parcel label was issued to the American Red Cross, Washington, D.C. That agency at the request of this office sent a package to your son in your name.

Sincerely yours,

Howard F. Bresee,
Colonel, C.M.P.,
Assistant Director,
Prisoner of War Division

**

On rare occasions correspondence from Grant Workman reached his family. A pre-printed postcard was sent to his sister on Imperial Japanese Army letterhead, presumably completed by him, date uncertain:

From Granville E. Workman

Nationality: American

Rank: Private

I am interned at: The Philippine Military Prison Camp #1.

174

My health is: excellent good fair poor

I am – injured; sick in hospital; under treatment; not under treatment

I am – improving; not improving; better; well

Re: family: Love to all

Please give my best regards to: all

**

In March 1945, Workman's family must have been overjoyed upon receiving a letter from him with no mention of the horrific conditions he continued to endure:

Tokyo CAMP 5-B

DATE 3/18/45

Dear Dad & Mom & Everyone, Well folks it gives me great pleasure to get to write home this morning. How is everyone? I hope everyone is fine. I am feeling pretty good.

Please write often as you can & send pictures, I get homesick every once in a while tell everyone I am well. Say, how is grandad & Mary? Tell them to write. This P.O.W. business is getting old, but I hope to be home soon. Give my best regards to all & good luck. "Till we meet again."

With lots of love,

175

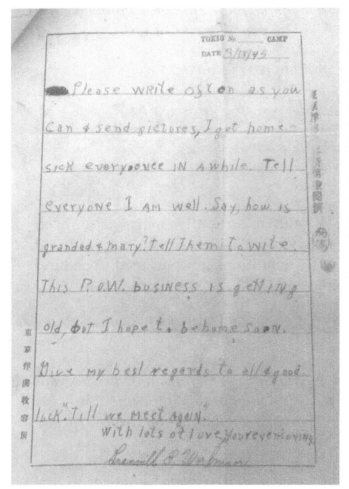

The second page of a letter from Workman to his family late in the war is hand-written on Japanese letterhead, issued to POWs.

The wording poignantly reveals the young man's desire to be done with the war and to go home. Notice the phrase, "This POW business is getting old."

"A person doesn't realize how important his freedom is until it's gone. It's the most important thing you will ever have."

-- Quote by Granville E. Workman in a story in the Bluffton News-Banner on May 15, 1992.

President Harry S. Truman announces Japan's surrender at the White House, Washington, DC, August 14, 1945. National Archives.

The following essay was written by Grant Workman many years after the war:

Three and a Half Years

A lot of people have asked me what it was like over there. My standard reply is 'three-and-one-half years is a long time even if you are having fun.'

Here are some of the things I did not have during this time.

1.   Never went to bed with a full belly!
2.   Never brushed my teeth, had no tooth brush or material to brush with
3.   Never had hope that to-morrow would be better than to-day
4.   Never heard a kind word from a parent or the love of another.
5.   Never thought until the last that I would get out alive.
6.   Never had any entertainment such as the free people had such as going to a movie, having a picnic, or just listening to a radio
7.   Never had a new pair of shoes or clothing
8.   Never had underclothes
9.   Never had medical attention

This list could go on. But the most important thing I never had was the desire to give up with one or two exceptions. One was after my bout with diphtheria, the other when we were worked nearly to death and cold and frozen in the northeast port of Niigata, Japan where we worked in the miserable coal yards. Three-and-one-half years where you had to live only one day at a time.

Lt. Gen. Jonathan Wainwright stands behind General Douglas MacArthur who signs as Supreme Allied Commander during formal surrender ceremonies. The ceremony took place on the USS MISSOURI in Tokyo Bay on September 2, 1945, thus ending the war with an Allied victory. Japanese representatives of Imperial Headquarters had already signed the surrender document. Wainwright was recently liberated after serving as a POW of the Japanese since Bataan. National Archives.

Aftermath of the Bataan Death March:

In 1942, upon being ordered by United States President Roosevelt to leave the Philippines, General Douglas MacArthur promised to return. He did so in October 1944, invading the island of Leyte. In February 1945, U.S.-Filipino forces recaptured the Bataan Peninsula and Manila was liberated in early March.

After the war ended in 1945, an American military tribunal tried Lieutenant General Homma Masaharu who had been in charge of the Death March. He was found guilty as it was considered a war crime and executed by firing squad on April 3, 1946.

Book Club Questions

1.   Compare lifestyles of the POWs in Europe with those in Japan. Did it seem as though one group had it easier? Why or why not?

2.   Several POWs attempted to escape. Which seemed to be more of a challenge – to be on the run from the enemy or a prisoner in a camp? Which would you choose?

3.   What part did religious faith have in the lives of these men as prisoners?

4.   How might news that your loved one was a POW affect your family?

5.   What would be your most challenging aspect of being a prisoner based on these stories – isolation from family, deprivation of food, clothing, sanitation, medical needs, other?

6.   How might the soldiers' lives after the war have been different if they had not been prisoners?

7.   What examples of positive thinking did the men implement? How did this help them survive?

8.   Should the author have left the scenes of brutality in the book or removed them?

9.   What do you take away from these stories about facing difficult circumstances?

10.   Did one particular story inspire you more than the others? If so, why?

World War II Timeline

1933

Adolf Hitler is appointed chancellor of Germany; the first of dozens of concentration camps over Europe is established at the German village of Dachau.

1938

Germany invades Austria; Hitler holds his last annual rally in Nuremberg, which draws one million people who support his practices and ideals.

1939

Hitler invades Poland and Czechoslovakia, causing both countries to surrender; Nazis begin persecuting Polish Jews; the United States sells military supplies to British and France to support their efforts to oppose the Nazis; Great Britain, Australia, New Zealand, Canada, South Africa and India declare war on Germany in fall, making this the official start to World War II.

1940

Germany takes over Denmark, Norway, Belgium, Netherlands, Luxembourg, and France; Winston Churchill becomes Britain's new Prime Minister; Italy joins the war with Germany; the Battle of Britain begins when Germany bombs London and other British cities -- the 'Blitz' continues on London for 57 nights, killing more than 40,000 citizens; Japan joins Italy and Germany in fighting the Allies; American president Roosevelt is elected to a third term, the only time an American president will serve more than two terms; Roosevelt bans racial discrimination in war-industry employment.

1941

Germany invades Greece; the United States continues to send military equipment and other supplies to the Allies with payment deferred until after the war; Germany attacks the Soviet Union; the Soviet Union joins the Allies; Japan attacks Pearl Harbor, along with other Allied bases in the Pacific and Asia, the result being the United States and Great Britain declare war on Japan; Germany and Italy declare war on the United States.

1942

The Nazis establish a plan to kill European Jews via death camps; Japanese troops take control of large portions of East Asia and the Pacific, including Hong Kong, Singapore, the Philippines, Thailand, Malaysia and Burma; United States invades North Africa; United States wins the Battle of Midway, a major turning point in the war in the Pacific; people of Japanese heritage are interned in the United States.

1943

Italy is invaded by the Allies and surrenders; Mussolini is removed from power; Italy begins secret peace talks with the Allies and eventually declares war on Germany; Churchill, Roosevelt and Stalin meet to discuss Operation Overlord, the Allied invasion of Normandy, France, against Germany's armed forces.

1944

In January General Dwight D. Eisenhower takes charge of planning Operation Overlord, which takes place in June; Allies push German forces towards Germany, liberating many cities including Paris; Roosevelt is elected to his fourth term as United States president; in December, the Germans attempt a last-ditch effort to overcome the Allies by splitting their troops, a strategy that becomes known as the Battle of the Bulge; Allied island-hopping in the Pacific liberates the Philippines.

1945

Prisoners at Dachau and dozens of other death camps throughout Europe are freed; Allies defeat the Germans in the Battle of the Bulge; Allies take the Pacific island of Iwo Jima; Churchill, Roosevelt and Stalin meet for the last time in Yalta to discuss the end of the war and how to divide Germany; in April Roosevelt dies and Vice President Harry S. Truman is sworn in as president; Mussolini is captured and executed by his own people; Hitler commits suicide in his underground bunker in Berlin; Germany surrenders in May; Truman declares the end of the war on May 8 as V-E Day (Victory in Europe); United States drops atomic bombs on the Japanese cities of Hiroshima and Nagasaki; the Soviet Union declares war on Japan; Japan's Emperor Hirohito accepts the Allies' terms of surrender on August 14, which becomes known as V-J Day (Victory over Japan); American troops begin returning home, while others are assigned to Japan and Europe during the Allied period of occupation. On September 2, 1945, the formal surrender occurs aboard the battleship USS Missouri in Tokyo Bay.

Excerpt from *It Was Our War Too: Youth in the Shadows of World War II*:

Johannes Klaffke

Running from the Russians

In the dark hours of January 19, 1945, a rumble was heard outside the village of Mehlsack in East Prussia. For months nine-year-old Johannes Klaffke, his six siblings and mother Anna had huddled inside their home, wondering who would reach their village first -- the Allies advancing from the west or Russians from the east. No matter who, the damage they would inflict was not to be underestimated.

During air raids over the past several months, the Klaffkes and their neighbors had watched in stunned disbelief as homes, businesses and other buildings, including the school where the Klaffke children attended, were destroyed.

Now, Johannes knew something even more sinister was approaching. The noise increased to a menacing growl as whatever it was neared the homes and businesses of Mehlsack. Suddenly an explosion ripped through the Klaffke's kitchen wall. Shards of glass from the window flew in all directions as the Klaffkes, clutching each other, cried out in fear. A Russian cannon ball landed in their midst.

The enemy had arrived.

Johannes' childhood had been peaceful. Even when Adolph Hitler took over Germany in 1933, Johannes' parents had not agreed with his punishment of Jews, special needs groups and gypsies, but caring for their 11 children had taken precedence over worrying about politics.

When Johannes' father, Albert, died in 1937, family members helped Anna and her children tend their farm, providing food and supplies. "Mother said she was glad Father was dead because he probably would have been thrown into prison for speaking out against Hitler," said Johannes.

After the attack on their home, Anna and her seven youngest children hurriedly packed their bags. They would head west, joining an estimated five million displaced Germans seeking refuge wherever it could be found.

Excerpt from *D-Day: Soldiers, Sailors and Airmen Tell about Normandy*:

George Banky – Navy/ Europe and Pacific

"It's not fun being fired on in the middle of combat," said George Banky of Waterloo, Iowa. "But that's what war is. You have to get yourself mentally fitted for it."

During the invasion of Operation Overlord, more commonly known as D-Day, Banky and 17 other sailors volunteered for a special mission with the Navy's amphibious force. It involved a flat-bottomed boat called LCF (landing craft flak).

"Our job was to go up and down the Normandy beach in an attempt to draw fire from the enemy during battle, said Banky. "We had small antiaircraft weapons but nothing big to defend ourselves. We were sitting ducks."

A horde of US naval destroyers, cruisers and battleships were positioned behind to help protect the smaller boat. During the heat of battle, the LCF cruised 24/7 for several days close to shore. "Shells hit the water around us and our boat was strafed, but thankfully, none of us were injured," Banky said. "Other seamen thought we were strange to volunteer for such a dangerous job."

Banky was born in Boston, Massachusetts, in 1926. He enlisted in the Navy at age 17 with his mother's permission as he was not yet 18.

After completing boot camp at San Diego, Banky was shipped to England in early 1944. He and thousands of other Allied troops trained for what scuttlebutt (military gossip) said would soon be a major invasion of US troops across the English Channel.

For once, scuttlebutt was true. The invasion of Allied troops on the beaches of Normandy, France, as part of Operation Overlord would someday become known as one of World War II's biggest battles.

About the Author

Kayleen Reusser has written about hundreds of veterans. As a speaker, she presents talks about her World War II tour of Europe to groups. For more information go to **www.KayleenReusser.com**.

Reusser's paperback books are available on Amazon. They can be purchased directly from the author, individually or as a set, signed and personalized. Contact the author through her website for bulk rates and set specials.

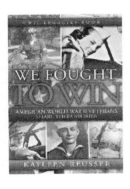

Made in the USA
Monee, IL
13 January 2021

57303630R00108